# DESIGNING
# FIELD EDUCATION

# DESIGNING
# FIELD EDUCATION

## Philosophy, Structure, and Process

*By*

## NINA HAMILTON

*and*

## JOHN F. ELSE

*School of Social Work*
*The University of Iowa*
*Iowa City, Iowa*

CHARLES C THOMAS • PUBLISHER
*Springfield* • *Illinois* • U.S.A.

*Published and Distributed Throughout the World by*
## CHARLES C THOMAS • PUBLISHER
2600 South First Street
Springfield, Illinois 62717

© *1983 by* CHARLES C THOMAS • PUBLISHER

ISBN 0-398-04863-0

Library of Congress Catalog Card Number: 87-4743

With **THOMAS BOOKS** *careful attention is given to all details of manufacturing and
design. It is the Publisher's desire to present books that are satisfactory as to their physical
qualities and artistic possibilities and appropriate for their particular use.* THOMAS
BOOKS *will be true to those laws of quality that assure a good name and good will.*

*Printed in the United States of America*
*Q-R-3*

*Library of Congress Cataloging in Publication Data*

Hamilton, Nina.
    Designing field education.

    Bibliography: p.
    Includes index.
    1. Social work education.   2. Field work
(Educational method)   I. Else, John F.
II. Title.
HV11.H326   1983              361.3′07′1              83-4743
ISBN 0-398-04863-0

to
our children

*Eve and Josh*
*Nathan and Nicole*

# PREFACE

THIS book has evolved over a period of two and one-half years in response to needs identified by those involved in field education at The University of Iowa School of Social Work. The book fills two major unmet needs in social work education: a systematic analysis of the philosophy and structure of field education, and a mechanism for facilitating and structuring individualized learning in field, namely, a practical guide for preparing learning contracts. Since some approaches to contracting are antithetical to humanist education, one section of the book is devoted to placing our approach to contracting within the context of humanist educational philosophy.

We express appreciation to The University of Iowa for the summer fellowships that supported the initial work on this book. We are indebted in a special way to The Iowa School of Social Work. We feel particularly blessed to be working in an environment that is so humanistically oriented, so cooperative, supportive, and stimulating. We appreciate the encouragement and critique of our work by faculty colleagues, field instructors, and students and careful preparation of the manuscript by the support staff of the school. We particularly thank Dixie Kramer and Pamela Lindley for their help.

We are especially indebted to Professor Katherine Kruse, director of practicum for the graduate program, who has been involved both locally and nationally for over twenty-five years in developing and refining the philosophy of social work field education and in designing and testing various innovations; her reflections, insights, assistance, and criticism have been invaluable. Our thanks also are extended to Professor H. Wayne Johnson, director of field experience for the undergraduate program, whose knowledge about and commitment to undergraduate education made him an invaluable source of information and a valuable reviewer of this manuscript.

We are also appreciative of our children, to whom this book is dedicated. They have taught us about learning, individualization, and empowerment, themes of this book. We are proud of them.

As coauthors, our areas of expertise — one micro practice and the other macro practice — complemented each other. We are fully coauthors. The ideas were developed in dialogue, and the writing and rewriting have taken us through a process that makes it difficult to attribute any single paragraph to one or the other of us. We are distressed by the complex norms of academia that offer no way to affirm this coauthorship, but insist on rankings of senior and junior, first and second. We reject such forced choices.

Finally, our own writing is consciously nonsexist. This is consistent with our personal commitments, as well as with the language policy adopted by The Iowa School of Social Work. Unfortunately, the works quoted often use the masculine pronoun when the reference is generic, and we have not found a readable way to correct for this.

N.H.
J.F.E.

# CONTENTS

Page

*Preface* . . . . . . . . . . . . . . . . . . . . . . . . . . . . . . . . . . . . . . . . .vii

*Chapter*

1. INTRODUCTION . . . . . . . . . . . . . . . . . . . . . . . . . . . . . . . . . . 3
   Field Education in Social Work. . . . . . . . . . . . . . . . . . . . . . . 3
   The Functions of Learning Contracts. . . . . . . . . . . . . . . . . 5
   To the Different Readerships . . . . . . . . . . . . . . . . . . . . . . . . 8

2. THE PHILOSOPHY AND STRUCTURE OF FIELD EDUCATION . . . . . . . 10
   Definition: What Field Education Is and Is Not. . . . . . . . . . . . 11
   Principles that Shape Field Education . . . . . . . . . . . . . . . . . . 13
   The Goal and Objectives of Field Education. . . . . . . . . . . . . . 17
   The Structure of Field Education . . . . . . . . . . . . . . . . . . . . . 23
   Options in Designing Field Education Placements. . . . . . . . . . . 32
   Other Issues. . . . . . . . . . . . . . . . . . . . . . . . . . . . . . . . . . . 46
   Conclusion . . . . . . . . . . . . . . . . . . . . . . . . . . . . . . . . . . . . 51

3. LEARNING CONTRACTS: RATIONALE AND ISSUES . . . . . . . . . . . . . 54
   Congruence with Humanist Education . . . . . . . . . . . . . . . . . . 54
   Potential Incongruence with Humanist Education. . . . . . . . . . . 61
   Related Research Findings . . . . . . . . . . . . . . . . . . . . . . . . . 71
   The Valid Contract: A Resolution . . . . . . . . . . . . . . . . . . . . 74

4. WRITING THE LEARNING CONTRACT . . . . . . . . . . . . . . . . . . . . 81
   Definitions . . . . . . . . . . . . . . . . . . . . . . . . . . . . . . . . . . . . 81
   Content. . . . . . . . . . . . . . . . . . . . . . . . . . . . . . . . . . . . . . 82
   Writing Goals . . . . . . . . . . . . . . . . . . . . . . . . . . . . . . . . . . 84
   Writing Objectives and Indicators . . . . . . . . . . . . . . . . . . . . 91
   Writing Learning Activities. . . . . . . . . . . . . . . . . . . . . . . . .109
   Writing Evaluation Plans. . . . . . . . . . . . . . . . . . . . . . . . . . .118
   Conclusion . . . . . . . . . . . . . . . . . . . . . . . . . . . . . . . . . . . .124
   *Name Index*. . . . . . . . . . . . . . . . . . . . . . . . . . . . . . . . . . .127
   *Subject Index* . . . . . . . . . . . . . . . . . . . . . . . . . . . . . . . . . .129

# DESIGNING
# FIELD EDUCATION

# Chapter 1

# INTRODUCTION

U nlike education in the humanities and social and physical sciences, professional education is preparation for practice. This requires that the educational design combine classroom instruction with instruction in the field, that is, in practice settings. Just as medical and dental students work in clinics under the supervision of practitioner instructors, and education students do practice teaching with classroom teachers, so social work students receive practice instruction from professionals in social agencies.

## FIELD EDUCATION IN SOCIAL WORK

There are many different views of the philosophy and purpose of field education, its place in the curriculum, and its design. As Valerie Garrard (1981) observed:

> Social Work educators appear to be ambivalent about fieldwork education. On the one hand, it is a significant component of most, if not all, social work curricula in terms of the time students spend in the field, the allocation of staff and other resources, and the impact of fieldwork on student learning. On the other hand, it is regarded as having dubious academic respectability as evidenced by the relative lack of attention paid to curriculum development in fieldwork compared to that accorded other parts of the social work curriculum, by the usually low status of fieldwork staff, and by the lack of interest in, and encouragement of, research in the area. (p. i)

According to Margaret Hamilton (1981), this ambivalence has resulted in field education being "undervalued and belittled. . . . Its status has been that of a necessary adjunct: that is, something added or attached, but subordinate" (p. 1). Hamilton argues that "fieldwork should be at the core of the total social work curriculum, the core around which other elements are constructed, with them dependent on fieldwork for their central reference and fieldwork dependent on them for a major part of its infrastructure" (p. 1).

The ambivalence of social work educators is matched by the confusion of students and agency-based field instructors. Students who enroll in social work programs tend to be "doers" — people who, anxious to engage in the practice of their chosen profession, are often impatient with the class-room courses. They may embrace the field component as a chance to "do" what they came to do. However, their previous academic experience gives them little frame of reference for conceiving of the field component as an educational endeavor that is planned, structured, and integrated into the total curriculum. They may conceive of it as nothing more than on-the-job training or work experience. For this reason, many students who return to school after holding social work positions have trouble understanding why all or part of the field education requirement should not be waived.

A different set of factors creates ambivalence among field instructors. They are usually social workers employed full-time by social agencies. Since they are seldom paid by the educational institutions, their teaching time is contributed by the agencies, which must justify the service time lost. Part of the instructors' time may be considered to be the agencies' service to the profession. The remainder is compensated for by the services students provide clients or communities while in placement. The pressure to recover lost service time may, unfortunately, lead field instructors and agencies to treat students in field placements as they would staff, to the detriment of the students' education.

Social work education suffers from this lack of clarity and consensus about the philosophy, purpose, place, and design of field education. Social work programs would be strengthened if these issues were addressed and decisions made that integrated field education into the curriculum more effectively and that more fully utilized field settings as teaching resources. Chapter 2 of this book addresses these problems by developing a coherent view of field education and analyzing the issues that are central to such a view. It then presents a framework for making decisions about the design of field education — a set of variables that must be considered in designing field programs and individual placements. The options within each variable are listed and some implications of the various options examined.

This book is written from a humanist educational perspective. Both the content and the process of education should empower students, that is, increase their self-confidence and self-reliance: by demonstrating respect for their worth and dignity; by encouraging them to be self-directing, and thus treating them as subjects rather than as objects; by having them participate in and share responsibility for their education; by making use of the richness of their experience; and by shaping learning opportunities around their felt needs. This educational philosophy is consistent with social work values, in the goal of empowerment and in the belief that the process must be congruent with the goal.

Since students disperse to a wide variety of placements, field education is inherently the curriculum component with the greatest degree of individualization and thus the greatest potential for implementing a humanist educational philosophy. In field education, a concerted effort can be made to merge the social work program's uniform expectations for educational outcomes with the personal goals of individual students. Chapter 3 explores the promise and the dangers of learning contracts as tools for implementing the humanist perspective in field education. The potential congruence between learning contracts and the humanist perspective is great, but it can be compromised if they are too narrowly conceived or are used to limit rather than to augment choice. We delineate seven characteristics that are essential to creating valid learning contracts, contracts that avoid the dangers while accruing the benefits of their use.

The final chapter presents in detail a specific format for learning contracts consistent with this orientation. It teaches the reader, through examples, exercises, and feedback, how to write such contracts.

## THE FUNCTIONS OF LEARNING CONTRACTS

Learning contracts can serve several important functions. Their use assures the educational focus of field, increases the likelihood of a good match of students and agencies/field instructors in the placement process, facilitates the educational process throughout the period of placement, and enhances the evaluation process.

First, the use of learning contracts requires students to ask the questions, "What does this program expect me to learn?" and rather than "Where do I want to do my field placement?" The development of a learning contract stimulates and structures discussion of program expectations and their rationale. Too often these expectations are simply imposed on and accepted by students. The absence of understanding and appreciation of program goals results in a lack of commitment to those goals and possibly a pretense of acceptance instead of honest dialogue about their meaning and significance.

Furthermore, students have seldom been asked to consider systematically what they want and need to learn, nor have they inquired about what faculty perceive as their specific learning needs. Learning contracts encourage thinking and discussion of learning goals and the development of a product that includes three perspectives — general objectives of the program, specific objectives of the student, and specific objectives of the faculty for the particular student.

The second useful function of preparing learning contracts is facilitating the selection of appropriate field placements. If all concerned are clear about what students want and need to learn and are aware of students' learning styles, various placement options can be assessed for the learning opportunities and the styles of field instruction they provide. Interviews between field instructors and students will be more fruitful, because specified objectives make it easier to determine whether the setting has or is willing to create and make available appropriate learning opportunities. Mutual exploration in the interview will give each party a sense of the other's personal style. This process increases the likelihood of a good student-instructor-agency match, which should result in a positive teaching/learning situation and relationship and thus a productive and enjoyable placement experience.

The third function of the learning contract is to obtain explicit commitments from all parties — agencies, field instructors, students, faculty, and educational institution. Agencies agree to provide specific learning opportunities; field instructors agree to provide particular instruction and evaluation; students agree to engage in certain learning activities over a given period of time; faculty agree to provide necessary and appropriate liaison, instruction, and evaluation; and the academic institution agrees to grant credit. The need to make explicit commitments sometimes encourages agencies to consider opening for students learning opportunities that have not previously been made available, and it sometimes encourages students to enlarge their vision of the learning activities they are willing to try.

Fourth, because contracts formalize commitments, they decrease the likelihood of misunderstandings or failure to achieve objectives. The contract spells out not only the expectations but also the criteria and process for assessing performance. Thus students are less likely to be "surprised" by expectations of which they were unaware or to be evaluated on unfamiliar criteria. While evaluation of performance in field placement inevitably involves many subjective judgments, the learning contract sets many parameters that limit the subjectivity of the assessment.

Finally, learning contracts provide a basis for mutual accountability. They provide grounds for any party to express disagreement or dissatisfaction with the progress of the placement. This is especially important for students, who are the least powerful participants in the educational enterprise yet are concerned to obtain the greatest value from their education.

One caveat: Learning contracts should not be considered unalterable. In some instances, student competence is greater than originally conceived, and learning contracts need to be expanded. In other instances, student performance indicates inadequate preparation for the level of learning specified, so the contract needs to be modified to reflect the level of learning for which the student is ready. Such modification should be made as joint agreements among the parties participating in the contract.

In addition to the usefulness of learning contracts in assuring an educational focus, good selection of placements, and a beneficial experience in the placement, preparing a learning contract is inherently educational. Students learn important practice skills. They learn to specify objectives and write them in outcome terms, to delineate requisite activities, and to design evaluation criteria and processes. These skills will serve them well in agency planning, grant writing, staff supervision, and making change contracts with clients.

## TO THE DIFFERENT READERSHIPS

This book is intended for *students*. It will help you get the most out of your field education. Learning about field education — defining it, understanding its place in the curriculum and the forms it may take — and then selecting goals and objectives and negotiating a learning contract may seem a burdensome and unnecessary chore. However, the process yields information and commitments essential to directing your education to meet your interests and needs. The learning contract is a tool to help you make useful choices for your own growth.

This book is also written for *faculty*. It seeks to clarify the philosophy and structure of field education, as well as various issues and options in its design. Thus it is a resource for the development of the field education curriculum. It is also a teaching resource for introducing students to field education and for facilitating joint planning and decision making.

You also may find burdensome the process of working with students in developing and negotiating contracts. But it is likely that you will increasingly appreciate the results. The clarity contracts provide and the intense interaction generated during their preparation set the stage for excellent working relationships and learning experiences throughout placement. Students will likely express greater satisfaction with their placements, and there will be less need for intervention to resolve problems. Using learning contracts concentrates into the early stages of placement much of the work that would otherwise be spread throughout the placement period.

We are also writing for *field instructors* and *agency executives*. Since effective field education depends on a partnership between agency and academic institution, it is critically important that, whether campus or agency affiliated, all those contributing to field education share a common understanding. This book provides a coherent and comprehensive overview of field education. It examines variables that agencies and field instructors have to consider in making decisions about field instruction commitments and lays out mutually exclusive choices within each variable.

The use of learning contracts in field education has a number of benefits for agencies and field instructors. The contracting process increases the likelihood of appropriate student referrals for placement; realistic and explicit commitments from students, field instructors, and agencies; and ease in evaluation.

## REFERENCES

Gerrard, V. Editorial. *Contemporary Social Work Education,* 1981, *4*(1), i-ii.

Hamilton, M. Fieldwork: The core of "academic" social work. *Contemporary Social Work Education,* 1981, *4*,(1), 1-13.

# Chapter 2

# THE PHILOSOPHY AND STRUCTURE OF
# FIELD EDUCATION

Field education is a universal component in undergraduate and graduate social work education programs. However it is titled — field work, field experience, field instruction, field teaching and learning, practicum, internship or field education — it is the component to which students in most programs devote the largest single portion of their time (Rothman & Jones, 1971, p. 45).

Field education carries academic credit. Programs vary, however, in the number of clock hours in the field that earn an hour of credit. Programs also vary widely in the number of credit hours of field education required. In 1980, according to Miriam Dinerman (1981, p. 56), the number of required credit hours of field in graduate and undergraduate programs varied from six to thirty. The credits given for field represented from 5 to 45 percent of the total social work credits required in BSW programs and from 14 to 40 percent of the credits required in MSW programs.

In spite of the fact that credit is earned, there is disagreement, first about whether field education is a "course," and second about whether a "field course" should have a syllabus prescribing objectives and content as is traditionally expected of classroom courses. As a result, students often receive no lectures, reading assignments, or other information presenting social work's definition of field education. Nor are students acquainted with the philosophy, assumptions, and principles that form the foundation of field programs. While most programs have handbooks that list objectives, they seldom include a presentation of these underlying issues.

What social work program or instructor would offer a classroom course without defining the subject matter and identifying the principles, issues, and approaches necessarily addressed in the study of that subject? Yet programs tend to neglect such an explication for this central course.

This chapter is an effort to remedy this deficiency. Subsequent chapters are designed to encourage and enable students to clarify and specify their personal goals within the framework of the larger purpose and objectives for the course. By implication, the book encourages students, faculty, and field instructors to see field education as a course — unique within the curriculum, but no less a course than any other component. As a course, it deserves attention to clarifying definitions, philosophy, and structure. This book provides a resource for field instructors and faculty members who have responsibility for directing, coordinating, and teaching field education.

## DEFINITION: WHAT FIELD EDUCATION IS AND IS NOT

Field education is a consciously planned set of experiences, occurring in a practice setting, designed to move students from their initial levels of understading, skill, and attitude to levels associated with autonomous social work practice. The field course has the advantage of not being restricted by either the intellectual isolation of the classroom or the unremitting pressures for action of practice. It allows for synthesis of the strengths of each through guided exploration, practice, and experimentation.

As an integral part of the social work curriculum, the content of field is shaped by the goals of the overall program. The course provides opportunities for students to test, integrate, and incorporate into their own practice the knowledge, skills, and values learned in the classroom. However, it is "misleading to assume that the classroom is where 'theory' is learned. . . and that field. . . is where the 'practical' side of practice is learned" (Maier, 1981, p. 14). Experiences in field at times deepen and at other times challenge the content of reading and classroom study. Through field education students develop and refine their conceptualizations and ways of thinking analytically about human behavior, societal structures, and social policies; the options for intervention; and their own practice.

Field education is distinguishable from job or volunteer experience in a desired arena of employment. It is not intended to provide agencies with short-term, unpaid staff persons. Its intent is educational.

Students will, of course, serve the clientele of the placement agencies. Educationally focused field education, however, must be guided by the aims of the program and the needs of students, rather than those of agencies and their clientele. Service to clients is, of course, an important by-product of field education, as well as a critical tradeoff for agencies providing instruction. The needs of agencies and their clients must be acknowledged and protected. But the educational focus of the field placement must always be affirmed as fundamental (see Dana, 1966; Hale, 1969).

This balance is upset if agencies treat students as regular staff members and give them full workloads for those portions of the week they are in placement. Under such circumstances, students do not have time to plan carefully, to do the reading and consultation required to prepare for their assigned duties, nor to reflect, assess, and critique their performances. Time for these activities is essential to the educational process.

Field education is also distinguishable from apprenticeship. Apprenticeship, in its best form, includes a broad education in a profession or trade. But is is frequently a narrower, more mechanical or technical preparation for employment. This more limited form of apprenticeship offers a useful contrast with the broader intent of field education.

Apprenticeship may be conceived as involving primarily "unconscious" learning or "emulation," whereas field education seeks "deep-rooted understanding and conviction" (Regensberg, 1966, p. 30). Apprenticeship emphasizes specific skills and procedures, whereas field education emphasizes the principles underlying skills and procedures. Apprenticeship puts low priority on generalizing from specifics. Field education places high priority on conceptual learning, whether inductive, generalizing from specifics, or deductive, learning general principles and concepts and applying them in particular instances (Schubert, 1965; Regensberg, 1966; Sikemma, 1968).

Apprenticeship "implies a fixed way of doing things in a situation that is viewed as static" (Schubert, 1969, p. 4). It implies "learning traditional, time-honored ways of performance without questioning their rationale or necessity" (Matson, 1971, p. 84). It assumes "stability in procedures and an absence of change in agency programs, policies, social needs, or the persons affected by the procedures," whereas professional education "recognizes change and uncertainty as a continuing fact of life" and prepares students to respond creatively to the shifting situations and demands they will face as professionals (Schubert, 1965, p. 40).

In the early years of social work education the apprenticeship pattern was used to prepare students for practice in a specific social agency, for example, an adoption agency, a settlement house, or a hospital. Current social work education seeks to prepare students for responsible entry into the social work profession. Field education·is designed so that learning can be generalized beyond the specific agency setting.

The contrast between apprenticeship and professional education may represent more of a caricature than a reality, but the distinction is useful for clarifying the nature and purpose of field education. On the other hand, much of what is learned in an educationally focused field placement results from the mentor-student relationship, particularly the modeling of professional practice. Sikemma (1966) acknowledges this when she discusses the dilemma of trying to "retain the values of apprenticeship learning" (p. 7) while assuring an educationally directed field program. Schubert (1969) notes:

> Certainly apprenticeship, if it involves an intimate contact with a curious and wide-ranging mind, should have many positives about it; there is no need to depreciate this form of learning when such contact is involved. In general, however, the effort to get away from apprenticeship in its less savory aspects involves a commitment to identifiable educational goals, with specification of curriculum content and desired outcomes. (p. 4)

## PRINCIPLES THAT SHAPE FIELD EDUCATION

Schubert's statement goes to the heart of the issue. The key to defining field education is recognizing that it is an *integral* part of the *total curriculum* of professional social work education. Field education is one mode of learning used in conjunction with classroom and independent study and research to achieve the aims of the program. Kindelsperger (1968) notes that the "modes are different only in the kind of involvement, physical and psychological, in which the adult learner finds himself, and not that of a dichotomy or a discontinuity between the modes of learning." He also assumes that "the modes are firmly connected on an interdependent scale and that in large part they are controlled by the same dynamics of learning" (p. 31).

The goal of field, then, like those of classroom instruction and independent study and research, must be determined by the goals of the total curriculum. The goals of the total curriculum are predicted on answers to basic questions such as "What is the purpose of the social work profession?" and "What sort of professional do we want to graduate?"

Eileen Blackey (1968) makes this point vividly in her reflections on a conference on field education. The discussion repeatedly shifted between specific aspects of the structure and content of the field curriculum and the larger issues of professional social work education. She wrote, "I recalled reading an entry the social worker made in a case record: 'Client kept interrupting the interview to talk about his problems' " (p. 60). In short, field education is not an end in itself and cannot properly be conceptualized or designed without repeated reference to the part it plays in the overall curriculum and thus in the preparation of people for service as professional social workers.

Once the purpose of professional education is identified, the next logical question is "What principles should guide the design of the field curriculum?" Three general principles of curriculum construction are regularly cited in the field literature: (1) continuity, (2) progression, and (3) integration. These are drawn from the broader education literature (Tyler, 1950, p. 55) and apply to the field course no less than to courses comprising the classroom component of social work education.

*Continuity* refers to the reoccurrence of major curriculum elements — concepts, theories, themes, issues, approaches, ways of thinking — in various forms in different components of the educational experience. For example, a systems perspective, a problem-solving approach, theories of social change, specific value considerations, and concern for self-awareness might be central elements of the total curriculum, both class and field. These would be considered in a variety of subject areas (e.g., human behavior, policy, research, practice) and in many different forms (e.g., readings, lectures, discussion, simulation and field practice). Continuity, then, is the provision of repeated opportunities for thinking, feeling, and doing related to each curriculum element.

*Progression,* or sequence, refers to the ordering of course content and learning experiences so that the expectations placed on students are for increasing levels of knowledge and skill and for behavior increasingly congruent with the values of the profession. These escalating expectations may include "new perceptions, new use of familiar materials, new adaptations of behavior (thinking, feeling, doing)" (Regensberg, 1966, p. 24) as well as "increasingly complex use of self by the student" (Simon, 1966, p. 408). Applying the principle of progression to the design of field education requires two decisions. First, when in the total curriculum design should the field course occur? Second, what ordering of learning in the field course itself will best prepare students for professional practice? Field education is the curriculum component that provides the necessary intermediate step in the progression from the classroom to autonomous professional practice.

*Integration* refers to the interrelatedness of the various curriculum elements and to congruence among thinking, feeling, and doing. It results from selecting and organizing content, resources, and experiences so that students identify relationships among the various curriculum elements. An integrated curriculum also leads students to discover perspectives and practice patterns (ways of thinking and ways of approaching issues and problems) consistent with their increasing sophistication. Field education is particularly conducive to integration because the interrelatedness of various concepts, theories, and themes becomes apparent in the process of applying them to practice situations.

Continuity, progression, and integration are useful in designing an educationally focused field curriculum. These principles are not sufficient, however, because of a number of circumstances unique to field education. For example, while a high degree of standardization of the structure and content of classroom courses is possible, the decentralization of the teaching and learning settings of field courses leads to much greater variation. These variations occur in the size and complexity of agency settings, in the types of service provided, in the approaches to the provision of services, in the styles of practice, in the backgrounds and orientations of the field instructors, in the responsibilities agencies and field instructors are willing to give students, and in the populations served.

These variations bring richness to the field curriculum. However, if social work education is to achieve its goal of preparing professionals equipped for autonomous practice rather than skilled technicians equipped only for one interventive mode in one agency setting, then the academic and field faculty must work together to assure that field settings serve the educational goal. Three additional principles have traditionally guided this effort: (1) equality of opportunity; (2) transferability; and (3) autonomy (cf. Sikemma, 1968, pp. 17-18).

*Equality of opportunity* means equity in the availability of basic, specified learning opportunities for all students. A field course syllabus specifying learning objectives provides a framework for discussion between program and agency to determine whether adequate opportunities are available for achieving those objectives. For example, providing equal opportunity may require that an agency assign students broader responsibilities than anticipated; provide experiences in more than one segment of the agency's work and/or with more than one staff person; supplement the experiences available within the agency with experiences outside; and, perhaps most important, focus primarily on educational needs and only secondarily on service needs.

Academic and field faculty have been creative in designing field education within an agency as well as in designing supplemental opportunities beyond the agency's practice boundaries. The equality of opportunity principle does not assume uniformity in field education. Students can achieve comparable educational outcomes within the framework of diverse experiences and settings.

*Transferability* means that what is learned is not limited to use in a particular agency or situation but can be generalized to other circumstances and settings. This suggests that field instruction must be conceptually oriented, helping students to identify the principles involved in practice and to make linkages with theory. Simon (1966) has said that what needs to be taught and learned is a way of thinking:

> To learn to analyze and assess his own professional performance in the light of his knowledge and understanding of the values of the profession — is essentially learning a way of thinking about practice . . . because a way of thinking about professional performance must have content beyond the details of one's own performance. A concentration on the details of one's own performance, unconnected to the basic substance of professional knowledge, may lead to a concentration on technical proficiency for its own sake. Furthermore, the major function of any educational endeavor is to establish a way of thinking that is tranferable to any content and any doing. (p. 399)

*Autonomy* refers to the development of student initiative, independence, and self-responsibility. This simply means that field education should be designed so that students become increasingly self-directed. To this end the field curriculum follows a progression of instruction. Students move incrementally, in accord with their practice competence, through the following learning sequence: observation, coparticipation, practice under direct (during service) instruction (see p. 42), autonomous practice with postservice review and instruction, and instruction of others.

## THE GOAL AND OBJECTIVES OF FIELD EDUCATION

The field component and the total educational program have the same overriding goal, namely, to produce effective social workers whose practice reflects the knowledge, skills, and values which define the profession. Field education makes two distinct contributions. First, it provides opportunities to test, integrate, and incorporate into one's behavioral repertoire the knowledge, skills, and values studied in the classroom. Second, it makes possible new learning that can happen only in the field and which then can be analyzed in the classroom to confirm, refute, or modify existing theory and methods. This section explicates the specific purpose of field education within the curriculum.

Various writers have defined the objectives of field education in different ways. Quotations from major authors convey the range of conceptualizations in the literature. Margaret Matson (1967) suggests five objectives for undergraduate field experience.

> Field experience is designed to help the student:
> 1. Gain first-hand knowledge and greater understanding of the network of social welfare services in the community. . .;
> 2. Gain an appreciation of the impact of such problems as delinquency, poor housing, family breakdown, and mental illness upon individuals, families, and communities;
> 3. Integrate and apply knowledge, theory, and understanding. . .;
> 4. Develop some of the techniques and skills common to practice in the social welfare field. . . ;
> 5. Become aware of and analyze his own value orientations and feelings about people and the problems they bring to social agencies. (p. 15)

Matson goes on to say that, in the achievement of these objectives, students should have opportunities "to assume responsibility for productive tasks within the agency; to observe and identify with the helping person in his various professional roles in the agency and community; and to assess his own interest in and suitability for a career in social work or in another helping profession" (p. 15).

Sikemma (1966) suggests that there are "two pivotal objectives" of field education: "affirming in performance the integration of thinking with feelings and values as a basis for professional activity; and affirming in performance a grasp of the underlying structure and significance of complex knowledge, of the connections among the parts of a whole" (p. 10).

Margaret Schubert (1965) identified four objectives: "skill in practice; skill in analysis of one's practice; self-awareness in the use of professional relationships; and the attainment of a sense of professional identity" (p. 44).

Bernice Simon (1966) developed and expanded Schubert's conceptualization into a set of five objectives.

> The student is expected:
> 1. To develop his ability to use knowledge for practice and to enhance his understanding of theory and principles;
> 2. To learn to analyze and assess his own professional performance in the light of his understanding of the values of the profession in order to establish a basis for continued, self-directed professional development;
> 3. To experience, learn, and incorporate the discipline and self-awareness necessary to the devleopment and use of purposeful pro-

fessional relationships;

4. To attain a sense of professional identity through understanding and incorporating professional values to control his practice;

5. To develop curiosity, a critical approach to theory and practice, receptivity to new ideas and the need to test them, concern for the way new knowledge has been obtained, and responsibility for continuous learning. (p. 398)

These and other formulations in the literature commingle goals, objectives, and subobjectives that represent different levels of generality. For example, Matson's third, fourth, and fifth objectives are general statements of knowledge, skills, and values, respectively. But the first two objectives — knowledge of social services and appreciation of the impact of social problems — are subobjectives. This intermixing of levels of generality in lists of objectives is the rule rather than the exception.

Another striking characteristic of the literature is the number of objectives that focus on linkages among knowledge, skills, and values. For example, Sikemma's first objective is integrating thinking, feeling, and values, and Simon's second objective is analyzing and assessing practice in the light of the knowledge and the values of the profession. In other words, in addition to objectives that focus separately on the incorporation of knowledge, skills, and values into one's own practice, there are objectives that focus on the need to integrate the three aspects into a *total concept of self as a professional* and into a style of practice that represents the best of what it means to be a social work professional.

This understanding leads logically to expanding the formulation of the overriding *goal of field education* to *the integration of knowledge, skills, and values into a concept of oneself as a professional and into a style of practice consistent with the knowledge, skills, and values that define the social work profession.* Thus the overriding goal of field education stresses the development of oneself as a professional social worker.

On the undergraduate level, students may not have had sufficient exposure to the profession to know what it involves and how they fit. For them, field education provides opportunities "to try out social work practice roles" (CSWE, 1971, p.18); "to observe and identify with the helping person in his various professional roles in the agency and community; and to assess his own interest in and suitability for a career in social work" (Matson, 1967, p. 15).

For both undergraduate and graduate students, the purpose of field education is the "attainment of a sense of professional identity" (Schubert, 1965, p. 44) and the development of "self-awareness as a social work professional" (Wedel & Press, 1977, p. 9). The concept of professional identity as presented here does not refer simply to self-image but to the integration and balancing of "the cognitive, affective, and relationship components of the professional social worker role" (McNew & DeYoung, 1970, p. 34).

## Knowledge Objectives

The overall goal can be discussed in terms of three categories of objectives — those related to knowledge, skills, and values. The knowledge objectives include all the thinking capacities: remembering previously learned material, comprehending meaning, applying learned material in new and concrete situations, analyzing material into its component parts, synthesizing material into new forms or wholes, and evaluating the worth of material for a given purpose (Bloom, Englehart, Furst, Hill, & Krathwohl, 1956). One set of knowledge objectives for field education emphasizes translating classroom content into practice and thereby gaining new understanding. This is central to the mission of professional education. As Charlotte Towle (1949) wrote, the "aim of professional education is to convey knowledge in such a way that the student may not merely possess it, but use it" (p. 140).

Authors use a rich variety of formulations to describe the relationship between classroom and field education. The following list (emphasis added) highlights this diversity. Through field education, students —

- develop "a *grasp* of the underlying structure and significance of complex knowledge, of the connections among the parts of the whole" (Sikemma, 1966, p. 10);
- develop "ability to *use* knowledge for practice. . .to *enhance his understanding* of theory and principles. . .*to analyze and assess* his own professional performance in light of his knowledge" (Simon, 1966, p. 398);
- "*illuminate, vitalize,* and *reinforce* social work concepts which are

dealt with theoretically in other parts of the curriculum" (McNew & DeYoung, 1970, p. 34);

- *"integrate* theory into practice behavior" (Wedel & Press, 1977, p. 9);
- *"integrate and apply* knowledge and theory and understanding derived from foundation courses" (Matson, 1967, p. 15); and
- *"test* in the field setting the theories and principles learned in the classroom" (CSWE, 1971, p. 81).

But the relationship between the classroom and the field is not unidirectional. Knowledge is not obtained solely in the classroom and then tested, reinforced, applied, integrated, vitalized, and used in the field. The field setting also provides new learning. The Council on Social Work Education's 1962 curriculum policy statement established the expectation that field education should enable students "to gain new knowledge and understanding, in all content areas of the curriculum" (CSWE, 1962). Thus field education should not only reinforce but also expand cognitive learning.

Margaret Matson (1971) gives examples of·"substantive knowledge" common in field education: "social legislation, . . .the network of community services, agency interrelationship, bureaucratic structure and functioning, and individual reactions to stress" (p. 87). She also describes the substantive knowledge which may be learned in given placements, e.g., "placement in a Model Cities program will probably add. . .to the student's knowledge of urban sociology, local government, and intergroup tensions," and placement "in a residential setting for the elderly would yield an understanding of social isolation; the significance of changes in social roles over a period of time, and Old-Age, Suvivors' and Disability Insurance and Old-Age Assistance Programs" (p. 87).

In addition to providing for the integration and application of classroom content and the acquisition of new knowledge, field education should promote a spirit of inquiry and a style of thinking. Koegler describes a major goal of education as "the development of a style of thinking which is inner-motivated, independent, and creative" (Koegler, Williamson, & Grossman, 1976, p. 34). Students in field education do not simply apply predetermined solutions to predictable problems. They must think creatively and respond effectively to situations and conditions that "do not quite 'fit' the models they have learned" (Koegler et al., 1976, p. 34).

Students are being educated to become autonomous practitioners, not trained to be technicians in an enterprise of human engineering. Thus they must learn to think for themselves — to seek and receive information, make assessments, and bring knowledge to bear on unpredictable situations. They must also acquire habits of continued learning which will assure familiarity with new knowledge as it develops in the field. The student must "develop a spirit of inquiry. . .that will not only sharpen his diagnostic skill but also will enable him to be aware of new problems and gaps in service" (McNew & DeYoung, 1970, p. 34). Or in Simon's (1966) words, one objective of field education is "to develop curiosity, a critical approach to theory and practice, receptivity to new ideas and the need to test them, concern for the way knowledge has been obtained, and responsibility for continuous learning" (p. 398).

## Skill Objectives

The skills of social work practice comprise the second category of objectives. There are several dimensions to these skills. Of primary significance is the general skill of *bringing knowledge to bear in a deliberate, planned problem-solving process.* Much of what is called social work practice is not the application of specific methods and techniques but the more general process described in the discussion of the knowledge objective, that is, the application or use of knowledge. Professional practice is not simply "doing" but understanding what one is doing — being able to give a rationale for the assessment made and for selecting one intervention from the numerous alternatives available.

A second general skill is referred to as *conscious use of self.* A cluster of interrelated skills, integral to all social work practice, comprise this capacity to know and to use one's own experience and abilities in the service of others. This cluster includes skill in observation of self, analysis of one's own practice, self-discipline, and self-disclosure. Professional practice thus requires initiative, independence, flexibility, and creativity.

A third important and pervasive dimension of skill to be learned or refined is the *development and maintenance of professional relationships* with one's colleagues and with the persons one serves. Finally, in addition to the three general skills, there are *specific practice strategies* (e.g., social action or family therapy) *and techniques* (e.g., news conferences, documentary research, making a family diagram, or reframing) to be learned, tested and practiced in field education.

## Values Objectives

The third objective concerns values. Field education gives students opportunities to become aware of and to analyze their own value orientations and their feelings as they interact with the people they serve, with their professional colleagues, and with social institutions. In this process students are led to affirm or alter their values and to increase the level of commitment to the values of the profession. They compare their values to those of the profession, judge their commitment to those values, express those values in their assessment of social policies and structures and in their own practice, and analyze and evaluate their own performance in light of those values.

Margaret Matson (1971) observes that students will discover both consistencies and inconsistencies between agency practices and professional values and will become aware of conflicts between social work and community values. A significant part of students' field education experience is sorting through the dilemmas raised by these realities and struggling to decide the stances they will take as each situation arises.

## THE STRUCTURE OF FIELD EDUCATION

Because field education is so central to the social work curriculum, and because social work educators are concerned that the field component be educationally focused, much attention has been given to determining its structure and placement in the curriculum design. The concern of educators has focused on four major issues: (1) *format,* whether to have concurrent or block field placements; (2) *timing,* when in the total educational process the field placement should occur; (3) *length,* how long the field placement should be; and (4) *number,* how many placements each student should have.

The decisions that each program reaches on these four issues are shaped by and have serious implications for its general educational philosophy, its philosophy of professional social work education, professional ethics, and the quality of service to clients or constituent groups served by the placement agencies. The choices available are also limited by practical constraints inherent in both the educational institution and the host agencies. These educational and practical concerns are complex and therefore not easily resolved. The following discussion presents some considerations that provide a basis for decisions on these issues.

### Format of Placement: Concurrent vs. Block

Classroom and field education can occur either simultaneously or sequentially. Concurrent placements follow a pattern whereby part of each week is spent in classroom courses and part in field education. Students enroll in class and field courses simultaneously. Block placements follow a pattern whereby classroom courses are taken in one "block" of time, and then a subsequent "block" is set aside exclusively for field education. While a block field placement may be the final segment of the degree program, it is more likely to be a middle phase, with additional classroom courses following the placement. Thus student enrollment follows the sequence of class, field, class. Some programs use what might be called a modified block placement system, where the field placement takes approximately four days a week for an intensified period of time with only minimal classroom work during the remainder of the five-day week.

The most common field education pattern in graduate social work education is concurrent field placements during both academic years of graduate study. This usually involves two days per week of field education together with three days of classroom courses during the first academic year and either two, two and one-half, or three days of field education combined with two days of classroom courses during the second academic year. Other programs have students in full-time course work for a least one semester followed either by concurrent or block placements.

Concurrent placements are also the most common format in undergraduate programs, although about one third use the block pattern (Boland & Johnson, 1978). The concurrent placements usually occur during the senior year, though some programs have placements during both junior and senior years. Block placements may be arranged for one semester of the senior year or for the summer preceding or following the senior academic year.

The same philosophic and pragmatic issues are involved in decision making at both graduate and undergraduate levels. Concurrent placement is favored by many social work educators on two major and related grounds. First, it creates the greatest potential for integration of classroom and field. Students who move back and forth regularly between the field and the classroom may have the best chance to test in the field those ideas, concepts, practice approaches, and skills learned in the classroom. They can also more readily bring their experiences and reflections from the field into the classroom, thus requiring classroom courses to face the immediate reality of the practice world. Integration is also fostered if academic faculty, knowing that all their students are simultaneously taking field courses, give assignments that can be done using the field setting as a resource.

The second argument is that concurrent placements tend to be more educationally focused. This is precisely because the student who is only present in the agency part-time is more likely to be treated as a student rather than an agency staff person. This promotes an educational rather than an apprenticeship orientation.

On the other hand, social work educators who favor block placements point to four major disadvantages of the concurrent format: limited placement options; missed opportunities for teaching and learning; interruptions in the provision of services; and potentially greater financial forfeiture for students. Proponents of concurrent placements see these as unfortunate but necessary trade offs for the greater integration and educational focus.

Concurrent field education limits the options for learning settings. This is both an educational and a pragmatic concern. Many colleges and universities with social work programs are located in rural areas with very limited choices for field settings. Block placements are essential if the program is to make use of geographically dispersed settings that provide a greater variety of learning opportunities for students. Block placements allow students to travel to more distant locations, since they do not have to be present in the classroom during the placement period. Similarly, social work programs in metropolitan communities may find that distance and travel time necessitate the block format for students whose educational goals require rural placements.

Another disadvantage of the concurrent arrangement is that students in field setting only two or three days a week miss occasions for learning. These opportunities are available only to students who are present four or five days a week. Certain assignments can only be given to students who are present the majority of the agency's work week. Activities related to the assignment may occur daily and need attention; an assignment may involve meeting regularly with a volunteer group or interagency task force that has a regularly scheduled meeting when the student is not in placement; or an assignment may involve staff persons who allocate certain days to that assignment, again when the student is not present.

Furthermore, many informal, unstructured opportunities arise in field settings. There are those events and crises that occur in agencies and provide serendipitous teaching opportunities for field instructors. These too may occur on days the student is not present. There are also informal but important networks of communication and association in agencies that are difficult for students to join, and this difficulty is exaggerated if they are not present essentially full-time.

In some settings, concurrent placements lead to interruptions or discontinuities in the provision of services. This is especially true in community organization and administrative placements where assignments demand daily attention and in agencies that provide short-term services. As an example, since much of the social work in community hospitals is with short-term patients, students who are present for only two days a week are not able to follow through with services to their assigned patients. This creates problems of continuity of care for patients. It also limits the learning of students who are unable to complete all stages of the service process.

Finally, the concurrent format has less flexibility for meeting the needs of part-time students. Block placements have been especially important in making part-time social work education financially feasible, especially for students who have extensive family obligations that limit the time they can be unemployed and devoted to full-time study. Although it sounds contradictory, block placement is usually more manageable for part-time students. Some part-time graduate programs are designed so that most of the classroom courses can be taken while students maintain full-time employment. Students leave their employment only for the semesters needed to complete the field education requirement, usually in block placements. This pattern is consistent with accreditation standards, which require a minimum of two full-time semesters of graduate study.

Given the advantages and disadvantages of each format, it is difficult to say that one is preferable for all students in all situations. One might ask, then, why programs need to make choices between these two forms rather than to make both options available. Ideally, the choice of format would be based on an educational philosophy that considers the learning styles and previous experience of students.

Some students' primary style of learning is experiential. They learn inductively, first engaging in experiences from which they can subsequently generalize to formulate concepts. For these students, the concurrent format best fits their learning style, because their conceptual learning is largely contingent on the experiential learning that occurs in the field. Other students' style of learning is conceptual. They learn deductively, first focusing on ideas and their interrelationships and only then applying and testing concepts in the field. For these students, the block format provides the best fit, because it allows them to immerse themselves in conceptual learning and to think through the implications for practice prior to moving into field education.

The differing backgrounds of students also have a bearing on the choice of placement format. Most undergraduates come directly out of high school with minimal life experience and no professional background. Other undergraduates are older persons with considerable life experience and sometimes even extensive professional or volunteer service. Similarly, graduate students may come directly from an undergraduate program and have little professional experience or enter a graduate program with a rich life and work history.

Those with little worldly or professional sophistication may benefit from concurrent involvement in field education to give them the missing experiential foundation to which they can relate their conceptual learning. Those with a rich background may benefit more from the block format, which allows an initial period of disengagement from professional activity so that they can reflect on, conceptualize, and integrate past experience into a solid theoretical framework.

## Timing of Placement

As indicated earlier, the most common pattern in graduate programs is concurrent placements for the entire two academic years. Thus placements and classes usually begin simultaneously. Sometimes the placement of first year graduate students is delayed a week or two to allow students to adjust to the program before being committed to a five-days-a-week schedule; this also allows field instructors to get the second year students underway before the first year students arrive on the scene.

Some graduate programs delay field education at least one semester, requiring that students take a minimum number of "core" courses before they begin field education. The intent is that students have some minimum base of knowledge, as well as some skill developed in a classroom or laboratory setting before being placed in a field setting. A conceptual foundation is critical to the educational focus of the placement, and beginning practice skill is critical for working with people seeking professional help.

By comparison, undergraduate social work programs are more consistent in their expectation that all students have certain minimal classroom experience before their field education. Field education usually occurs in the senior year, although in some programs it may occur in the spring semester of the junior year or as a block placement in the summer following the junior year. Other programs mandate field education in both junior and senior years.

In addition to the field education course, many undergraduate programs have built into their curricula a variety of volunteer experiences, sometimes even in the introductory social work course. These volunteer or observational experiences allow some acquaintance with the profession and some early evaluation of this career choice for undergraduates who are unfamiliar with social work. This exploration makes it less likely that students will suddenly discover during field placement — often during the senior year when a change of major means prolonging their education — that social work is not for them. Another pattern being followed in some undergraduate programs is to have limited, specifically focused field, assignments as one of the requirements in classroom courses on practice methods. These field assignments provide exposure to, and sometimes limited practice in, specific methods while students are learning the principles and processes of those methods in the classroom.

## Length of Placement

There has been much debate about the minimum amount of time that should be spent in field education. The actual length of placement varies widely among programs. Accreditation standards effective July 1984 specify a minimum of 400 clock hours (equivalent to 50 eight-hour days) of field education for undergraduate programs and 900 clock hours (112.5 eight-hour days or 120 days of 7.5 hours each) for graduate programs (CSWE, 1982a, p. 12). Some programs just meet these minimum standards, while others require significantly more than the standards dictate.

Dinerman (1981) reported that for undergraduates, field education requirements in 1979 varied from 40 to 104 days. Since her figures were calculated on the basis of a seven-hour day, the undergraduate program requirements (when the accreditation standard was 300 clock hours) ranged from 280 to 728 hours. Graduate program requirements, according to Dinerman, varied from 120 to 365 days (840 to 2,555 hours).

According to the 1982 "Summary Information of Master of Social Work Programs" prepared by the Council on Social Work Education (1982b), the number of days of field education required by graduate programs varied from 90 to 306 days. The most common requirement, that of 37 percent of the 81 graduate programs for which clear data was available, was 120 to 129 days. Another 38 percent require between 130 and 169 days. Thus three fourths of the programs have requirements within the range of 120 to 169 days. Only one program requires more than 200 days, and only nine less than 120.

This variation in length of placement reflects different perceptions of the time required for achieving the objectives of the field course. It is difficult to predict, specify, or generalize about the length of time required to complete the many learning activities necessary to reach the objectives. Students must have both a diversity of experience and enough repetition of key elements to develop practice competence. They must be present in the setting long enough that their increasing competence can be demonstrated and the agency can then make assignments that demand greater responsibility and autonomy. Some learning activities involve one-time, short-term assignments; others involve a prolonged series of similar experiences; still others necessitate longer assignments requiring several months to complete.

In addition, agencies have a "life cycle" of planned activities and predictable crises, so that participation over a several month period is required in order to experience the full range of activities and agency responses to crises. The complexity of the factors to be considered in deciding length of placement is obvious. Decisions can only represent educated judgments.

Additional factors make the problem even more complex, namely, individual differences among students. Students begin field education with differing levels of knowledge and skill, and they learn in different ways and at different rates. This reality raises questions about whether there should be a uniform requirement for length of placement even within a single program. Since the difficulty of making such fine distinctions is enormous, most programs have a uniform requirement. Some programs do make provision for students to reduce the length of field placement on the basis of previous field education or work experience. Sometimes the decision is not made until after the student has begun field education, so that it can be based on an assessment of the student's actual level of performance rather than simply on a transcript or work record. Some programs make provision for extension of time in placement if a student has not demonstrated a minimal level of competence. Thus the length of placement can be individualized, within program constraints, to fit student needs.

## Number of Placements

The typical choice that programs make is to have either one or two placements. As indicated earlier, the most typical graduate program pattern is two different concurrent placements, one each academic year. Sometimes graduate programs have only one, longer placement. Undergraduate programs also vary. Those which require only the minimum number of field education hours are likely to have only a single placement, but other programs are designed with two.

The major argument for two placements is that learning opportunities are broader when there are placements in two distinct settings and with different practicum instructors. On the other hand, proponents of single placements argue that breadth is possible. A single placement can include a diversity of field instruction as well as participation in various programs and services of the agency. The agency may make supplementary learning assignments outside the agency as part of the placement.

A single placement provides a longer period in one setting and thus a greater depth of experience and increased opportunity for responsibility and autonomy. In some graduate programs, the majority of students enter with considerable social work experience. They are acquainted with various social work settings. Therefore depth is more important to them than breadth, especially if the placement is designed to build on rather than duplicate their prior experience.

On the other hand, since undergraduates have less acquaintance with the range of social work settings and the work that occurs in each, breadth of experience is a higher priority and provides a rationale for two placements rather than one. The same argument could be made for graduate students with no prior social work experience.

Practical issues affect the choice of number of placements. For example, schools that have block placements may choose to have only one placement on the grounds that the total length of time in field education is too brief to make orientation and integration into two different field settings feasible. Similarly, if a graduate program delays entry into field education for one or two semesters, the remaining time for either concurrent or block placements may be too brief to make two settings productive. Lastly, if a program wants to make use of learning opportunities in placements some distance from campus, a single off-campus placement, with all the attendant disruption of students' lives, is much more practical than two such placements.

## OPTIONS IN DESIGNING FIELD EDUCATION PLACEMENTS

As we have seen, many options exist for incorporating field education into the overall curriculum design. Even more choices are available for designing the field education program itself and the specific placements. The typologies in the literature are variations on three basic patterns: agency placements, teaching centers, and service centers (see Jones, 1969, pp. xiii-xiv; and Sikemma, 1968, pp. 19-20). These typologies focus on only one dimension — that is, the administrative structure and location of the field placement — to the exclusion of many other significant dimensions on which decisions about field education design may depend. Thus the typologies tend to obscure the extensive options available.

On the other hand, a comprehensive typology, one that lists all dimensions and all combinations and permutations, would be excessively cumbersome and confusing. Thus this section steers a middle course. Eighteen dimensions along which decisions must be made when designing field education are identified, and options or choices available within each are listed. These eighteen dimensions fall into three major categories: (1) the *learning opportunities* available in the placement; (2) the source and kind of *field instruction;* and (3) the *characteristics of the field instructor.* Following the listing of the dimensions and options is an explanation and discussion of the variables within each.

### *Learning Opportunities*

1. Administrative Structure and Location
   a. agency

    b.  teaching center

    c.  service center

    d.  campus

2.  Field of Practice or Social Problem Area

    a.  one field of practice/social problem area

    b.  multiple fields of practice/social problem areas

3.  Theoretical Orientation of the Agency

    a.  one theoretical perspective

    b.  two or more theoretical perspectives

4.  Methods of Practice

    a.  one practice method

    b.  one primary, other secondary methods of practice

    c.  multiple practice methods with relatively equal emphasis (generalist orientation)

5.  Interdisciplinary Potential

    a.  social workers only

    b.  limited interdisciplinary exchange

    c.  extensive interdisciplinary teamwork

6.  Primary Service Area

    a.  rural

    b.  small city

    c.  metropolitan area: inner city

    d.  metropolitan area: suburban

7.  Diversity of Population Served

    a.  service assignments exclusively or primarily with people of one group, e.g., age, class, race, sex, religion

    b.  service assignments with people of diverse groups

8.  Breadth of Service Assignments

    a.  one unit of one agency

    b.  several service/program units of one agency

    c.  primary assignment in one agency with supplementary assignments in other agencies

    d.  coordinated multiple agency assignments

9.  Potential for Student Innovation

    a.  work only with existing client groups using existing service approaches

    b.  develop alternative service approaches and/or extend services to new constituencies

*Field Instruction*

10. Source of Field Instruction
    a. single (exclusive) field instructor
    b. primary instructor plus secondary (supplementary) instructors
    c. multiple instructors
11. Number of Students Jointly in Placement
    a. one
    b. two to five
    c. teaching unit of six to twelve students
12. Teaching Format
    a. individual conferences
    b. group sessions
    c. both individual and group
13. Teaching Methods
    a. direct (during service) instruction only
    b. post service instruction only
    c. both direct and post service instruction

*Field Instructor*

14. Theoretical Orientation of Field Instructor
    a. one theoretical perspective
    b. one primary theoretical perspective with understandings and techniques from other perspectives integrated into practice
    c. several theoretical perspectives
15. Education and Experience as Practitioner
    a. BA in social work with limited or extensive specialized training, professional experience, professional standing
    b. MSW plus limited or extensive specialized training, professional experience, professional standing
    c. degree in another discipline plus social work experience or orientation with limited or extensive specialized training, professional experience, professional standing
16. Education and Experience as Field Instructor
    a. no formal education in field instruction and limited expe-

rience as an instructor
  b.  no formal education in field instruction and extensive experience as an instructor
  c.  formal seminar in field instruction and limited experience
  d.  formal seminar in field instruction and extensive experience
17. Field Instructor's Employer
  a.  agency
  b.  educational institution
18. Time Committed to Field Instruction
  a.  full-time
  b.  part-time

## Learning Opportunities

1. ADMINISTRATIVE STRUCTURE AND LOCATION. The traditional, and still most common, field education setting is an existing social service agency. A second type of setting is the "teaching center." Teaching centers are established by social work education programs. They are independent of any single agency. This makes possible the design of a coordinated set of assignments in several different agencies, and, on occasion, in the community, not linked to any specific agency program or project. Some teaching centers are neighborhood or community based, while others are organized around social problems or fields of practice. Some centers are housed in existing agencies but are clearly defined as operating independently; others are housed in their own quarters and are both physically and administratively independent.

"Service centers" are a third type of setting. They are essentially new agencies created by social work education programs specifically, but not exclusively, to provide education for students. They are analogous to the laboratory schools operated by colleges of education or teaching hospitals operated by medical schools. While service centers provide social work services to people, they are designed with a predominantly educational focus.

Finally, some field placements are campus based. Faculty members located on campus serve as field instructors for students. Assignments may be related to a single community project or may consist of a variety of experiences with several different agencies and organizations.

2. FIELD OF PRACTICE OR SOCIAL PROBLEM AREA. Many agencies in which students are placed are involved in intervention in one or more social problems such as crime, unemployment, poverty, physical and mental illness, substance abuse, family violence, racism, sexism, aging, or neighborhood deterioration. They may also provide services in one or more fields of practice, such as health, mental health, corrections, child welfare, family intervention, civil rights, or housing.

A setting that initially appears narrow in its focus may offer involvement in a wide spectrum of issues, since social problems generally do not occur in isolation. Intervention in the case of family violence, for example, often reveals related problems of substance abuse, economic dependency, and illness. There are times, however, when learning may be restricted by the way an agency defines and limits the scope of its intervention.

3. THEORETICAL ORIENTATION OF THE AGENCY. Student knowledge can be greatly broadened, deepened, or restricted by the fit between an agency's theoretical stance and student learning needs. Some agencies deliberately create a variety of program units and select their staff to assure diversity in theoretical orientation to change, including the system level addressed, as well as in practice methods and techniques. Other agencies operate a single program, adhere to only one orientation, and hire only social workers of like mind..

Agencies with multiple theoretical approaches offer a breadth of practice experience that is especially critical for beginning students and those whose aim is to broaden their practice orientation and skills. Agencies with a single theoretical orientation restrict the learning opportunities for such students but could be ideal for students with solid generalist skills and extensive social work experience who wish to become immersed in a single specialized approach.

4. METHODS OF PRACTICE. Social work programs conceptualize methods of practice in different ways. Some use the triad of casework, group work, and community organization. Others use the dichotomous formulation of micro and macro practice. Still others depart from these traditional approaches in favor of other conceptualizations such as ecological models (Baer & Federico, 1978; Germain, 1973; Meyer, 1970; and Pincus & Minahan, 1973). Whatever conceptualization is used, the question for field education is what

the placement provides: education in only one method, in one primary method with others secondary, or in several methods with relatively equal emphasis.

5. INTERDISCIPLINARY POTENTIAL. Social work staff in some settings have contact with professionals from other disciplines only in connection with referrals or other interagency business. Staff in other settings have regular interdisciplinary contact, but the exchange is limited. Social service department staff in a community hospital, for instance, will interact daily with doctors, nurses, and other professionals but may have little significant exchange.

In hospitals and other settings with multidisciplinary staff, such as mental health centers, residential treatment centers for youth, area education agencies, and regional planning organizations, there are either patterns of limited exchange or extensive interdisciplinary teamwork. Each profession may operate independently in its own domain or may function as part of an integrated team, bringing the expertise of various disciplines together in a concerted effort, jointly developing and implementing plans. The diversity of disciplines at work in the setting and the nature of the work relationships can make important contributions to student learning.

6. PRIMARY SERVICE AREA. Agencies ordinarily have a primary geographic focus for their services. They serve a rural area of villages, small towns, and the surrounding farming area; or small cities of 50,000 to 200,000; or metropolitan communities of several hundred thousand or a few million. In metropolitan communities, services are likely to be directed either to the low-income, inner city populations or to the middle- and upper-income, suburban populations. Some agencies will serve both constituencies, sometimes through branch offices in different areas of the city. Regional agencies, such as education agencies that provide services to schools in multicounty areas, may have only one location, but the primary assignment of staff is to serve either urban or rural schools.

7. DIVERSITY OF POPULATION SERVED. The diversity of the population served by a placement agency depends first of all on the field of practice or social problem on which it focuses. That is, a council on aging will serve almost exclusively the elderly, a runaway shelter will serve adolescents, a Jewish Community Center the Jewish community, a hospital the ill, a battered women's shelter women and

children, a civil rights organization minorities. Certain settings automatically place limitations on the chance to work with certain populations.

Within these restrictions, assignments can be shaped to maximize contact with more diverse groups. As an example, one emphasis in programming for the elderly is intergenerational exchange; therefore, a student could potentially interact not only with elderly of all races, classes, sexes, and religions, but also with different age groups.

Similarly, agencies that serve adolescents may include programming for parents, or organizations focusing on minority rights may include programming for majority groups that addresses their racism, sexism, or other bias.

The primary concern, then, is not the agency's target population but the scope of its programming and thus the diversity of populations from which students can learn. In some cases, however, an agency that has a broad scope of service may have a fairly narrow service constituency — it may actually serve only one ethnic, religious, or economic group. Alternatively, an agency that has a highly specific service focus may reach a diverse population.

8. BREADTH OF SERVICE ASSIGNMENT. In some agencies, students work exclusively in one service or program unit: for example, in an early childhood development, counseling, or community organization unit of a family service agency, or in a psychiatric, rehabilitation, or family practice unit of a community hospital. Other agencies design a rotation or a split assignment among their service or program units to provide broader exposure to the range of social work practice occurring there.

Still other agencies plan student involvement in outside assignments for those forms of service not provided by the agency; for example, a family service agency could arrange part of the student's placement assignment in an information and referral center, a crisis center, or a neighborhood organization project. Finally, a social work program might arrange varied assignments in multiple agencies and provide coordination from an independent "teaching center."

9. POTENTIAL FOR INNOVATIVE STUDENT ACTIVITIES. Some agencies expect students to confine their involvement to existing

client groups and established service approaches. Other agencies see the students' presence as an opportunity to expand the present agency parameters and thus are accepting or even encouraging of student efforts to extend services to new constituencies and/or to try out new approaches.

### Field Instruction

10. SOURCE OF FIELD INSTRUCTION. The number of field instructors involved in the education of an individual student will determine the nature of that student's field education. A single field instructor offers intensity and depth, but limited breadth and diversity. Multiple instructors bring breadth and diversity at the price of depth.

If a student has one field instructor for the entire placement, an intense relationship involving individual conferences and tutorials is likely. The instructor will become a mentor who acquires some depth of knowledge and understanding of the student. This familiarity may result in pressing the boundaries of the student's competencies to maximize growth, or it may make it difficult for the field instructor to make the demands and critical assessments essential to the continued growth and development of the student.

An intense relationship could lead to varied assignments and a clear explication of the connections among them, or it could result in a very narrow set of experiences directly related to the interests and skills of the field instructor. It can foster dependency on the suggestions and advice of the instructor, or it can nourish the growing autonomy of the student. Which of these outcomes occurs depends largely on the orientation and educational philosophy of the particular field instructor. When the field instruction is the responsibility of a single instructor, how broad the experience, how integrated, how shaped by the student's own style, is heavily dependent on the views and approach of that person.

If there is one primary field instructor with secondary (supplementary) instruction by other staff persons, students are exposed to different practice and teaching styles. The secondary instruction may come from staff engaged in the same service unit as the primary instructor or in different units of the agency. A student whose field instructor is in the community organization unit of a family service agency may be assigned to another organizer who has a somewhat different philosophy and style than the primary instructor. The secondary instructor will have insights into the student's practice and will be able to raise questions and make suggestions different from those of the primary instructor. (This is analogous to the function of the three faculty members on a thesis committee; each has a different contribution to make for improving the draft and suggesting other resources.) The same student may be assigned to the agency administrator, to the agency's grant writer, or to a case worker. In such cases, the educational potential is broadened. It remains the responsibility of the primary field instructor to help the student integrate those experiences into a unified understanding of social work practice.

A third option is multiple field instructors without the designation of one as primary. This pattern occurs when field education is designed as a set of learning modules, each of which is to be guided by the person responsible for that aspect of the agency's program. Students may progress sequentially through the modules; or they may divide their time each week between two (or more) learning modules; or some combination of sequential and simultaneous learning may be arranged. Although this pattern insures that the most knowledgeable persons provide instruction, integration is left to the student. Field instructors may help with the integration process, but no one is specifically charged with the task.

Finally, some placements necessitate a division of instruction between a faculty member and an agency staff person. A common circumstance leading to this arrangement is the absence, in an agency or organization that can provide outstanding learning opportunities, of a field instructor who meets the criteria of the social work education program. In order to use the placement, an arrangement can be made for daily supervision of the student by agency staff and field instruction by a faculty member familiar with the work of the agency who maintains close contact with the agency-based supervisor.

This arrangement gives students learning opportunities that are otherwise unavailable, while assuring that field instruction is educationally focused and social work oriented. The major drawback is that instruction is provided by a person who is not intimately involved in the daily work of the student and whose knowledge of the structures and interaction patterns of the agency is inevitably limited. The student often benefits from dual instruction, since educational instruction is, in fact, provided by the agency-based supervisor who does not formally qualify as a field instructor by the social work education program standards.

11. NUMBER OF STUDENTS JOINTLY IN THE PLACEMENT. It is common practice for one student to be placed in a setting. Particularly if the one student has one field instructor, the instructor-student relationship is likely to be intense and to emphasize modeling the behavior of the instructor. This arrangement raises concerns about the breadth of learning and the potential for dependency rather than autonomy of the student (McNew & DeYoung, 1970, p. 31; Sikemma, 1968, p. 18). On the other hand, it could be argued that having only one student in the setting encourages a quantity of attention from other staff as well as the field instructor that is likely to result in intensive interactions and thus heightened learning.

The practice of jointly placing two or more students not only lessens the intensity of the instructor-student relationship but has the advantage of creating a support group to relieve the considerable anxiety students experience, particularly in the early stages of field education. Having other students on site also supplies another important source of learning, namely, the knowledge and perceptions of one's peers (Schubert, 1965, p. 45; Sikemma, 1968, p. 18).

A "teaching unit" of 6 to 12 students creates yet another situation. One staff member is assigned full-time as field instructor to a group of students. The relative autonomy of this "unit" may interfere with student integration into agency structure. On the other hand, the field instructors are more likely to see their primary function as teaching and thus to generate assignments that more directly meet the educational needs of students.

12. TEACHING FORMAT. The choice of teaching formats is closely related to, but nonetheless distinct from, the choice of the "number of students jointly in the placement." The issue is whether teaching is done via individual conferences, group sessions, or a combination of the two. If only one student is in the placement, the individual conferences format may be the only alternative. Some field instructors choose the individual conferences format even when two or more

students are in placement. Other instructors with two or more students may use only group sessions and not individual teaching conferences. As discussed above, there are both benefits and costs associated with an intense one-to-one relationship with the field instructor. Different benefits and costs are associated with group instruction. Perhaps the best alternative is some combination of the two teaching formats.

13. TEACHING METHODS. Some field instructors arrange the learning environment so that they can directly instruct students during the delivery of service. They observe student work in progress and intervene directly with immediate feedback and instruction at the time rather than after the fact. In one form of direct instruction the teacher is present in sessions as an auxiliary practitioner. The primary responsibility for conducting the session is the student's. The instructor intervenes only to redirect or to assist with information gathering or intervention and then withdraws to the secondary role.

In another form of direct instruction the student conducts a session in a room equipped with one-way glass or closed-circuit television; the instructor observes from an adjacent room and communicates with the student by telephone or intercom connection. Direct instruction then takes the form of comments, suggestions and directives about interventions the student is making or might make. The instructor may enter the room to intervene directly or the student may leave the session for consultation.

In both forms of direct instruction, the teacher is the social worker in charge, responsible for overseeing the service delivery and the case, project, or program planning. The student is responsible for conducting and reporting the entire social work process. The teacher is a "resource person" who guides the student's preparation and occasionally redirects the interventive process or models practice behavior.

Postservice instruction is more common. It is used exclusively, or as a supplement to direct instruction, since it is less demanding of field instructors' time. In this teaching method, completed practice experience is reviewed. The instructor critiques performance and guides student self-assessment and planning for future intervention. Alternative interventive approaches, theoretical perspectives and assumptions, ethical implications, and personal concerns are considered.

The review is based on reported practice experience. Reports may take various forms: videotapes, audiotapes, process recordings, verbatim reports, summary reports, statistical reports, or the actual documents that are the products of assignments. Postservice instruction is not the exclusive province of the field instructor. It may also be received from other students or agency staff during staff meetings, staff development sessions, case or project staffings, or field education seminars.

In settings where direct instruction is provided in the field placement, there is usually a shift over time toward less direct and more postservice instruction. This progression encourages and acknowledges the student's movement toward more autonomous practice. As students mature professionally, there is increasing opportunity for them to offer other students postservice and even direct instruction as members of a collegial team.

### Field Instructor

14. THEORITICAL ORIENTATION OF THE FIELD INSTRUCTOR. Since all practice models are founded on particular theories of human behavior and change, dysfunction and growth, the theoretical orientation of field instructors has a major impact on students' practice learning. A field instructor who understands human struggle from a psychodynamic perspective will guide students toward different assessments and interventions than an instructor whose world view is behaviorist or systemic. An instructor strongly committed to one orientation may work exclusively from that perspective or may integrate into practice understandings and techniques from other perspectives. For some students, teaching from several different field instructors, either within the same agency or in additional placements, will guarantee the breadth of learning that meets their educational needs.

15. EDUCATION AND EXPERIENCE AS PRACTITIONER. Field instructors vary in formal and informal education and in length, diversity, and quality of employment experience. Some programs require that all field instructors hold MSW degrees. Others allow experienced BA social workers and professionals from other disciplines

who have extensive experience in social work or who understand and share a social work orientation to serve as field instructors. Independent of formal education, the amount and kind of continuing or specialized education completed by instructors varies. Some instructors have regularly attended brief workshops on specialized topics, and others have completed extensive postgraduate programs in specialized areas of practice. Training programs with no formal educational prerequisite may still be judged to contribute highly to practice excellence; for example, a community organizer may have taken a six month or even two year training program taught by Alinsky's protegés.

Experience as a practitioner may vary in the total years of service, in the number and kinds of positions held, and in the number and kinds of agencies in which the instructor has practiced. Also, instructors who have made contributions beyond agency boundaries may be in leadership positions and have professional standing that creates exceptional learning opportunities. For example, an instructor who holds office in the regional association of medical social workers or of a regional NASW chapter can make specific assignments related to those activities.

Instructors vary in education, formal and informal, in diversity of experience, and in professional standing. All of these educational and experiential factors come together to influence and form field instructors' knowledge, skill, and general competence as practitioners and thus what they have to teach field students.

16. EDUCATION AND EXPERIENCE AS FIELD INSTRUCTOR. In addition to differences in education and experience as practitioners, field instructors vary in the amount of specific preparation they have for teaching. Many educational programs provide, and some even require, a seminar in field instruction. While some education and background in supervision is beneficial, field instruction is distinct, and practitioner instructors need education specifically focused on the principles and problems involved. The variations among instructors in the number of years of teaching experience, the diversity of students taught, and the educational issues they have confronted may be significant factors affecting a placement choice.

17. FIELD INSTRUCTOR'S EMPLOYER. In most cases, field instructors are employees of the agencies in which students are placed.

They are well respected and well integrated into agency structures. They can open doors to diverse learning opportunities and can interpret for students the political and interpersonal processes of the agency and its programs and services. Their stake in the agencies as employees, however, may prevent field instructors from being as critical of agency philosophy, policies, and processes as less engaged persons might be. Agencies also have the right to make certain demands on employees' time, which may on occasion require instructors to place lower priority on teaching than either they or their students would prefer.

Field instructors employed by academic institutions were more prevalent in the late 1960s and early 1970s. At that time federal grants were readily available for experimenting with new patterns of field instruction, and colleges and universities were not under the financial constraints that characterize the 1980s. Even though there are fewer field instructors employed by educational institutions today, they do still exist. Such arrangements have been strongly promoted because they assure an educational focus. Assignments are based on the learning needs of students rather than on the needs of the agency. They have been favored also for their greater promise for integrating classroom and field instruction. A faculty member familiar with the total curriculum will, as a field instructor, be committed to facilitating class and field integration.

The inherent difficulty with this arrangement is that a field instructor can seldom be both fully a faculty member and fully an agency staff person. Full-time field instructors often have marginal status on the faculty and in the agency. If the agency considers the field instructor an adjunct staff person the result may be less student access to certain learning opportunities. If, in addition, the instructor is not in the agency full-time, he or she may not be present to facilitate the education that occurs through the crises and unpredicted events arising in the life of an agency.

18. TIME COMMITTED TO FIELD INSTRUCTION. For most field instructors, teaching is one responsibility among many pressures and demands placed on them by their agencies or academic institutions. Even though they may find field instruction stimulating and satisfying, the inescapable reality for part-time field instructors is that lower priority is placed on teaching than either the students or in-

structors think appropriate. On the other hand, it is precisely their active engagement in practice that makes part-time field instructors valued social work educators.

Though they are relatively rare in the 1980s, there are still some full-time practicum instructors. Their attention and commitments are less divided, and therefore they are more able to focus on providing the best possible field education for students. We have already noted the potential costs associated with employment as a full-time field instructor.

## OTHER ISSUES

To close, three additional issues are discussed which are central concerns for field education: Where is the locus of control of field education? What is the process for making placement decisions? How are academic faculty involved in field education?

### Educational Responsibility

Implicit in much of the discussion of this chapter are questions about the locus of responsibility for, authority over, and control of field education. The perspective throughout this chapter has been that field education is one part of the social work curriculum and thus is shaped by the overall goals of the program. It follows, therefore, that the educational institution is ultimately responsible for the field program: for determining the objectives, for setting standards and criteria for instruction and student performance, for implementing the program, and for evaluating the performance of field instructors and students (Blackey, 1968, p. 63; Dana, 1966, p. 59; Sikemma, 1966, pp. 12-13). Educational programs must carry out this responsibility. Rigorous education is essential to assuring well-qualified graduates who enter the profession able to work effectively with colleagues and clients.

Field education, however, requires a partnership between educational institutions and service agencies which necessarily brings with it compromise between the needs of the agencies and the goals of the educational program (Briar, 1972; Dana, 1966; Hamilton, 1981).

To carry out their share of the educational responsibility, field instructors must be acknowledged as partners. They must be consulted on the design of field education, that is, curricular issues (such as the objectives, standards, and evaluation criteria), administrative processes, and specific placement decisions. If field instructors do not participate in the planning and decision making about field education, they cannot be expected to have either the information or the commitment essential to the effective implementation of curricular goals.

### Placement Processes

Placement decisions range from faculty making the decisions either arbitrarily or with minimal information from or consultation with students to giving students primary responsibility for locating and negotiating their placements. Between these extremes are various alternatives that involve the faculty, students, and field instructors in joint decision making.

One approach to making placement decisions is a system for matching students and agencies using data collected from both. Questionnaires are given to students asking them to specify their learning objectives and the learning opportunities and settings they prefer. Agencies are asked to complete questionnaires describing the characteristics of the agency, such as its purpose, services, personnel, practice methods, and population served as well as the learning opportunities available. The faculty then make placement decisions by "matching" student interests and characteristics with the characteristics of the placement settings. Some programs have even developed a computerized "management information system." Data from questionnaires are coded, and matching is done by computer. In describing one such system, Brownstein (1981) argues that it retains individualization in the placement process and, at the same time, significantly reduces the time spent in decisionmaking.

When programs have several hundred students to place and a hundred or more placement settings, a computerized matching process may, in fact, provide more individualization than would more arbitrary decisions made by faculty or staff persons who cannot possibly know all students personally. In graduate programs where students begin placement soon after arrival on campus and before thay are known to faculty, such a process may do a better job of matching than would otherwise be feasible. One shortcoming of this process is the absence of direct contact; there is no matching of students with agencies and field instructors on style and affective variables.

At the other end of the spectrum of placement processes are programs that expect all students to find and negotiate, with assistance from the program's placement director, their own placements, including arrangements for field instruction (Fortune, 1982). The program may provide a list of possible agencies (though students can go beyond such a list) and must approve the arrangements. This approach maximizes student initiative and the mutuality (program, agency, and student) of the placement process. (To assure equal opportunity, all students negotiate placements within a specified time period.)

This approach also increases the probability of a "match" on the personal level, as well as agreement on learning objectives and opportunities, since the process involves direct interaction between students and their potential field instructors. Such a match is important if the relationships between students and field instructors are considered critical elements of the educational experience. It should be noted that this process is virtually impossible for graduate programs in which first year placements begin with the start of the first semester of classes. However, it is feasible for second year placements and for graduate programs where placements begin in the second semester or later. Though logistically workable for most undergraduate programs, this process assumes a level of knowledge, experience, and maturity beyond that of many undergraduate students.

A third placement process combines certain elements of the two approaches described above. It works best for second year graduate placements, for programs where placements do not begin until at least the second semester, and for undergraduate programs. It could work, however, even for first year concurrent graduate placements if there were a one month delay in starting placements during which decisions could be made.

This process begins with an orientation to the philosophy and purpose of field education and the general objectives of the particular field program. Students are assisted in thinking about and writing out additional or more specific objectives for their field education. The faculty then presents students with data gathered from various placement settings and subjective data from faculty experience with the placements and instructors.

By matching the specified learning objectives (the program's and the individual student's) with the data (objective and subjective) on the learning opportunities in agencies, students select three to six settings they wish to explore. Faculty review student lists to assure congruence. In instances where there is no congruence, student and faculty conferences are necessary. When congruence is achieved, faculty approve the list and give students permission to contact instructors. Each field instructor is sent a list of those students who wish to explore that placement. Students are responsible for making their interview appointments.

The field instructor may hold individual or group interviews or some combination of the two, but no commitments for placement are made. Following the interviews, students give faculty a rank-ordered list of their placement preferences and field instructors give faculty a rank-ordered list of the students. Faculty then make placement decisions based on the preferences of the various parties as well as the perceived learning needs of the students.

This process assures a match between learning objectives and opportunities based on three sets of data: written data provided by the agencies, subjective data provided by faculty who have coordinated placements, and personal interaction between students and field instructors. The process provides opportunity for mutual interviews of students and field instructors, thus increasing the chances of a good match on the personal level also. In spite of its advantages, the complexity of this process might make it unmanageable for very large programs.

Another idea adopted by some programs to increase efficiency and reduce complexity is the "agency fair." Field agencies send representatives to a central location on a specified day. Students are provided in advance with written materials describing the agencies. At the "fair" students and agency representatives (most of whom are field instructors) interact to obtain more detailed information and to form impressions of each other.

The various placement processes are attempts to individualize placements. Decisions on how to do this must take into consideration both the philosophy of the program and the various practical constraints under which it operates.

## Direct Faculty Involvement in Field Education

The academic faculty determines the educational objectives and the criteria for assessing outcomes. It sets criteria for the selection and evaluation of field instructors. It decides the place field education will have in the comprehensive curriculum design, how the content of the social work program will be divided between classroom and field, and how the two will be integrated into a coherent whole.

Of central import is whether the involvement of most faculty members is limited to conceptualizing and making policy decisions or whether they are also engaged in the decisions and activities of field education. Will they have direct responsibility for arranging placements, for liaison with field instructors and students, for teaching of field seminars, or for designing and implementing seminars for field instructors?

In some programs these functions are assigned to faculty members recruited and hired specifically for these purposes. Other programs distribute these duties among faculty members. Frequently these assignments are assumed by different faculty members in rotation. In some of these programs, the coordination or liaison function is distributed so that *all* faculty members participate. In other programs, responsibility for placements and coordination/liaison is rotated among several faculty members. Several faculty members may take responsibility for teaching a field seminar or for providing instruction in placements where there is no qualified field instructor.

Decisions about the allocation of responsibility for field instruction have significant implications for the status of field education within the curriculum. If it is delegated to faculty specifically hired for that purpose, it tends to have a lower status in the curriculum. The faculty members responsible for field education often occupy lower academic ranks and sometimes even hold adjunct, non-tenure-track positions. In these cases the message is clear, that field education is not considered as central and as critical a part of the curriculum as classroom teaching. In contrast, when senior faculty have responsibility for field, or when the functions are shared among all or a major portion of the faculty, the message conveyed is the importance of this curriculum component.

How responsibility is allocated also has implications for the integration of the curriculum. If a small, segregated segment of the faculty has total responsibility for field, field and classroom cannot possibly be as well integrated as when most of the faculty, either regularly or intermittently, share responsibility for both.

## CONCLUSION

This chapter presented a number of issues that must be addressed when designing field education. It presented options for consideration in making decisions about the shape that field education will take, both for programs and for individual students. The assumption that underlies the discussion is that there is value in individualizing education as much as possible within the context of general objectives and expectations established by social work education programs. In order to facilitate such individualization within programmatic constraints, this text advocates the use of learning contracts in field education.

## REFERENCES

Baer, B.L., & Federico, R.C. *Educating the baccalaureate social worker.* Cambridge, MA: Ballinger, 1978

Blackey, E. Summary: Observations and questions about structure. In Council on Social Work Education, *Field learning and teaching: Explorations in graduate social work education.* New York: Council on Social Work Education, 1968.

Bloom, B.S., Englehart, M.D., Furst, E.J., Hill, W.H., & Krathwohl, D.R. (Eds.). *A taxonomy of educational objectives: Handbook I, the cognitive domain.* New York: David McKay, 1956.

Boland, M., & Johnson, H.W. Survey of undergraduate field instruction programs. Unpublished study, 1978. (Available from H. Wayne Johnson, The University of Iowa, School of Social Work, Iowa City, Iowa.)

Briar, S. Practice and Academia. *Social Work,* 1973, *18*(6), 2.

Brownstein, C. Practicum issues: A placement planning model. *Journal of Education for Social Work*, 1981, *17*(3), 52-58.

Council on Social Work Education. *Official statement of curriculum policy for the master's degree program in graduate professional schools of social work.* New York: Council on Social Work Education, 1962.

Council on Social Work Education. *Undergraduate programs in social work: Guidelines to curriculum, content, field instruction, and organization.* New York: Council on Social Work Education, 1971.

Council on Social Work Education. *Curriculum policy for the master's degree and baccalaureate degree programs in social work education.* New York: Council on Social Work Education, 1982. (a)

Council on Social Work Education. *Summary information on master of social work programs.* New York: Council on Social Work Education, 1982. (b)

Dana, B. The role of national agencies in stimulating the improvement and expansion of field instruction resources. In Council on Social Work Education, *Field instruction in graduate social work education: Old problems and new proposals.* New York: Council on Social Work Education, 1966.

Dinerman, M. *Social work curriculum at the baccalaureate and masters levels.* New York: Silberman Fund, 1981.

Fortune, A.E. Teaching students to integrate research concepts and field performance standards. *Journal of Education for Social Work*, 1982, *18*(1), 5-13.

Germain, C. The ecological perspective in casework practice. *Social Casework*, 1973, *54*, 223-230.

Hale, M.P. Innovations in field learning and teaching. In B.L. Jones (Ed.), *Current patterns in field instruction in graduate social work education.* New York: Council on Social Work Education, 1969.

Hamilton, M. Fieldwork: The core of "academic" social work. *Contemporary Social Work Education*, 1981, *4*(1), 1-13.

Jones, B.L. Introduction. In B.L. Jones (Ed.), *Current patterns in field instruction in graduate social work education.* New York: Council on Social Work Education, 1969.

Kindelsperger, W.L. Modes of formal adult learning in preparation for the service professions. In Council on Social Work Education, *Field learning and teaching: Explorations in graduate social work education.* New York: Council on Social Work Education, 1968.

Koegler, R.R., Williamson, E.R., & Grossman, C. Individualized educational approach to fieldwork in a community mental health center. *Journal of Education for Social Work*, 1976, *12*(2), 28-35.

Maier, H.W. Chance favours the prepared mind. *Contemporary Social Work Education*, 1981, *4*(1), 14-20.

Matson, M.B. *Field experience in undergraduate programs in social welfare.* New York: Council on Social Work Education, 1967.

Matson, M.B. Field experience for undergraduate social welfare students. In L.J. Glick (Ed.), *Undergraduate social work education for practice: A report on curriculum content and issues.* Washington, D.C.: U.S. Government Printing Office,

1971.

Meyer, C.H. *Social work practice: A response to the urban crisis.* New York: Free Press, 1970.

McNew, E., & DeYoung, A. Field instruction at Marywood: It's micro, macro, and modular. *Journal of Education for Social Work,* 1970, *6*(1), 29-40.

Pincus, A., & Minahan, A. *Social work practice: Model and method.* Itasca, IL: Peacock Publishers, 1973.

Regensberg, J., Report of exploratory project in field instruction. In Council on Social Work Education, *Field instruction in graduate social work education: Old problems and new proposals.* New York: Council on Social Work Education, 1966.

Rothman, J., & Jones, W. *A new look at field instruction.* New York: Association Press, 1971.

Schubert, M.S. Curriculum policy dilemmas in field instruction. *Journal of Education for Social Work,* 1965, *1*(2), 35-46.

Schubert, M.S. An overview of field instruction: Making the best use of traditional and atypical field placements. In B.L. Jones (Ed.), *Current patterns in field instruction in graduate social work education.* New York: Council on Social Work Education, 1969.

Sikemma, M. A proposal for an innovation in field learning and teaching. In Council on Social Work Education, *Field instruction in graduate social work education: Old problems and new proposals.* New York: Council on Social Work Education, 1966.

Sikemma, M. The symposium: Historical prologue. In Council on Social Work Education, *Field learning and teaching: Explorations in graduate social work education.* New York: Council on Social Work Education, 1968.

Simon, B.K. Design of learning experiences in field instruction. *Social Service Review,* 1966, *40*(4), 397-409.

Tyler, R. *Basic principles of curriculum and instruction.* Chicago, IL: University of Chicago Press, 1950.

Towle, C. The classroom teacher as practitioner. In *Social work as human relations.* New York: Columbia University Press, 1949.

Wedel, K.R., & Press, A.N. Expectations for field learning: An initial assessment. *Journal of Social Welfare,* 1977, *4*(1), 5-14.

# Chapter 3

# LEARNING CONTRACTS:
# RATIONALE AND ISSUES

This chapter sets forth the usefulness of learning contracts for promoting both humanist educational philosophy and social work values. It also analyzes potential problems, reviews relevant research, and delineates the characteristics of valid contracts.

What is a learning contract? It is an agreement, collaboratively designed by student (learner) and teacher (facilitator), that specifies intended educational outcomes, teaching/learning resources and methods, and evaluation processes for a given educational unit (cf. Berte, 1975, pp. 3-4). Learning contracts are widely used to individualize education. There is an extensive literature on contract learning. Much attention was focused on the process in the 1960s, when the "open classroom" became popular in elementary and secondary schools and when "experimental colleges" emerged within private and public institutions of higher education.

## CONGRUENCE WITH HUMANIST EDUCATION

Learning contracts received attention in part because they provide a mechanism for implementing a humanist educational philosophy — a philosophy that advocates active participation of learners in the design of their education, that treats learners as subjects rather than as objects, that acknowledges students as responsible, self-directed independent persons, and that values and makes use of the richness of their past experience. This humanist orientation to education is reflected in the progressive education philosophy of John Dewey (1916, 1934), in the adult education philosophy of Malcolm Knowles (1970), in the socio-political writings of Freire (1970) and

54

Illich (1971), and in the popular writings on education by Coles (1967), Goodman (1962), Holt (1964, 1969), and Kozol (1967, 1972).

## Humanist Orientation in Adult Education

Malcolm Knowles (1972) draws a distinction between "pedagogy," the art and science of teaching children, and "andragogy," the art and science of helping adult learners. He notes that "all the great teachers of ancient history — Lao Tse and Confucius in China, the Hebrew prophets, Jesus, Socrates, Plato, Aristotle, Euclid, Cicero, Quintilian — were chiefly teachers of adults, not children" (p. 33). Knowles observes that the great teachers assumed learning was a process of discovery, and they used procedures, dialogue, and "learning by doing that were consistent with that assumption. It was only in the Middle Ages that these teaching approaches came to be labeled "pagan" and were forbidden in monastic schools.

> As novices were received into the monasteries to prepare for a monastic life, it was necessary that they be taught to read and write if they were later to use and transcribe the sacred books. The teaching monks based their instruction on assumptions about what would be required to control the development of these children into obedient, faithful, and efficient servants of the church. (p. 33)

According to Knowles, *pedagogues* "have traditionally decided what knowledge and skills needed to be transmitted to students and then have developed lesson plans or course outlines. . .for transmitting them." On the other hand, *andragogues* "define education not as a process of transmitting knowledge but as a process of inquiry — mutual, self-directed inquiry. They concern themselves, therefore, with preparing and marshalling resources for engaging learners in inquiry according to *process designs,* and they define their role as facilitators and resources in the process of inquiry" (p. 36).

Knowles (1972, pp. 34-36) presents four assumptions about the adult learner from which he draws four principles of andragogical theory that differentiate it from pedagogy: (1) Maximum learning occurs when the educational expectations are consistent with the learner's self-concept as a self-directing adult. (2) Since adult learners have rich life experience, which can be analyzed and drawn upon as learning resources, the educational expectations should place "decreasing emphasis on the transmittal techniques of traditional teaching and increasing emphasis on experiential techniques which tap the experience of the learners and involve them in analyzing their experience" (p. 35). (3) Since adult readiness to learn is the product of the developmental tasks required for the performance of evolving careers and social roles (they are ready to learn those things they believe they need), learning opportunities should be shaped to recognize those needs. (4) Since adults seek education primarily to cope more adequately with current life problems and want to apply immediately what they learn, the curriculum design should be problem centered.

## Humanistic Education: The Empowerment of Learners

Many educators stress the need to respect learners' dignity and worth and to encourage self-direction. Adelman and Taylor (1977), for example, argue that "What the learner views as worthwhile and something she can do should be the first concern of the person who wants to facilitate learning." Too often, "the very process of schooling has taught them not to trust their own perceptions of what is worthwhile and what they can do effectively" (p. 457). In short, education often creates dependency rather than enhancing independence and self-direction by helping learners realize their capacities and develop confidence in their abilities and judgments.

In calling for "liberation in social work education," Thomas Brigham (1977) refers to Paulo Freire's position that education either oppresses or liberates. Freire envisions a world "in which people create their own reality" and suggests that education designed to empower people requires that learners be subjects, not objects; that the learning process be a two-way, horizontal dialogue in which the "teacher" takes the role of "facilitator" or "coordinator" in a partnership; and that learning be a process of critical reflection-action, a merging of critical thinking (knowledge), action (skills), and consideration of social and political implications (values).

Hokenstad and Rigby (1977) urge application of these concepts to social work education. They call attention to the need for consistency between *what* is taught and *how* it is taught. If we are teaching social workers to be facilitators of problem-solving, then educators should model the facilitator role.

> There is an educational model that gives students the central role in the teaching-learning transaction and that is more appropriate for social work training. Learning is produced through the interaction of the students with their environment and students have an active role in the learning process. The teacher creates the opportunity and structure for learning by performing the role of catalyst — a facilitator of learning rather than a transmitter of knowledge. (p. 6)

Adelman and Taylor (1977) also emphasize the relationship between the teaching-learning approach and what students learn. They observe, "By using power, whether grades, money, size or age to coerce someone else to behave in ways we decide are best, we are participating in oppressive behaviors. Our behavior is an important expression of our values and our beliefs about others, and is a better teacher than our words" (p. 460).

They argue that the socialization effect of an authoritarian approach to teaching contributes to the formation of attitudes that perpetuate current class, race, and sex prejudices and barriers and help to maintain the status quo "at considerable expense to the process of learning and the people involved" (p. 460). They maintain, "The role of the facilitator of learning is one of leadership within the learning environment. Whether a teacher influences behavior through leadership or through power has major socio-political significance" (p. 460).

Colby (1978) notes that the capacity for self-reliance is developed by individualizing education through contracting. The process of negotiating a learning contract requires learners to think carefully and to identify their "capacities, interests, and personal qualities" (p. 22).

Similar points are made by Flanigan (1974), Gilbert (1976), and Hartwig (1975). Flanigan observes that when social work students stipulate their own change goals and progress through the phases of a change plan, they experience their own competence and an increased incentive to change (learn). Hartwig notes that the individualized approach in a counseling and guidance degree program gave students opportunities "to use imagination, problem solving and creative skills" and encouraged "students' responsibility for their own learning. . ." (p. 16). And Jay Gilbert, describing the experience of the Empire State College program, which functions entirely with learning contracts, states —

> Planning a contract is, in itself, a learning experience. Students must think about their own goals, the relevance of the area being considered for study, the objectives of the college, and perhaps the changing needs of a profession. . . .Another educational advantage of contract learning is the ability to assist students to become capable of self-directed learning. (p. 29)

Thus an educational program shaped by a philosophy of empowerment and liberation gives students experience in the same processes they are urged to implement in their social work practice. Regardless of the terminology used — self-reliance, self-determination, or "maximum feasible participation of the poor" — a central concept of social work, whether with individuals, groups, or communities, is to help people develop their own capacities to identify their problems, to establish problem-related goals, and to focus action on change. Just as contracting is one way to transform the teacher-student relationship from that of giver-receiver to one of active collaboration in the problem assessment and change process, so also can the social worker-client role be transformed.

### Humanistic Education: Learning for Use

As noted earlier, Knowles, Freire, and others place great emphasis on the importance of shaping learning opportunities around the felt needs of the learner — of assuring that learning is for use (praxis). Motivation and excitement about learning are greatly increased when the learner can appreciate the importance and the relevance of what is to be learned. Hockenstad and Rigby (1977) note that social work education is "preparation for use" — that the "central task of the social work educator is not only to help students learn theory and techniques but to help them acquire skill in applying this knowledge to social problem solving" (p. 10). Thus the very purpose of social work education is learning for practice, but the linkage between what is being learned and how it is used in practice is not always apparent to the student nor explained by the teacher.

Both the format and the process of negotiating learning contracts contribute to understanding the importance and relevance of the learning. Since the format relates each learning objective to specific learning activities (and vice versa), connections between tasks and objectives are explicit. Furthermore, the process of negotiating and developing contracts increases the likelihood of extensive communication between learners and facilitators. Students identify their learning needs and desires and provide a rationale for experiences to reach those objectives. Instructors explain elements of the social work curriculum and their relevance for practice.

Increased clarity of the rationale for the objectives established and a clearer understanding of linkages among these objectives, curriculum areas, and learning experiences facilitates attainment of educational goals. In sum, contracting results in a clearer formulation of the "ends of social work education" and "the nature of practice" (Westbury, 1978) and moves toward what Houpt, Weinstein, and Russell (1977) have called a "unified explanation of what is frequently seen as a random set of experiences" (p. 296). (See also Cleghorn & Levin, 1973.)

## Benefits of Learning Contracts

A variety of benefits of learning contracts — to students, to the learning process, and to student-teacher relationships — are cited in the literature. For example, students know what they have committed themselves to; there is a written record; students can better plan their time; there is greater motivation to learn; there is communication and feedback at regular intervals; there is a sense of progress and satisfaction as segments of the contract are completed; the selection of teaching content, materials, methods, and experiences is facilitated; and the basis for evaluation of the achievements of the learners and the effectiveness of instruction is specified.

One author (Berte, 1975) summarizes the advantages of learning contracts as increasing student autonomy, initiative, involvement, and responsibility; developing student skills in persuasion and negotiation; fostering cooperative student-teacher endeavors and an "intellectual advisor role" (rather than a parental role) for faculty; encouraging interdisciplinary studies; and better utilization of the total learning resources of the community.

In short, using learning contracts is consistent with theories of learning, expresses the values of the social work profession, and prepares students for professional practice reflecting those values. While our brief discussion of Knowles and Freire touched on theories of learning, study of Bruner (1966), Dewey (1916, 1934), and others (e.g., Bigge, 1964; Hilgard & Bower, 1966) lends support to the principles of individualization and learner participation as major contributors to successful learning (for a discussion of the application of learning theory to social work education, see Sommers, 1969, 1971; Tyler, 1961).

The model of student-teacher partnership expresses and provides practice in cooperation and mutuality, values of a society in which we share responsibility for each other's well-being. It expresses the principles of cooperation, democracy, and egalitarianism. It encourages the practice of leadership based on expertise and persuasion rather than on authority and power.

Unfortunately, there are common misconceptions about learning contracts. One such misconception is that students unilaterally determine what and how they will learn. While learning contracts are formal mechanisms to assure learner *participation* in decisions about learning objectives, they are *mutual* agreements and not mechanisms for shifting unilateral decision making from teachers to students. As Knowles (1972) puts it,

> I don't see the final objectives as consisting exclusively of those the students perceive to be important. The student's self-perceived objectives are certainly the starting point, but I believe that I as a teacher have responsibility to add to the list those objectives I believe are important and that my institution, the profession, and the larger society identify as being important. The final list of objectives is achieved by negotiation between the students and the teacher. (p. 38)

Learning contracts are particularly appropriate for use in field education for two reasons. First, field education is the course in which practical application of learning is most central. Second, it is already the most flexible and individualized component of the social work curriculum. Contracts can provide a mechanism for structuring and specifying this often nebulous component. In classroom courses, a single set of objectives is usually established for all members of the class. This is not possible in field education, where students are dispersed to a variety of agencies offering diverse learning opportunities. The diversity of student interests and goals and the diversity of opportunities available in the field necessitates tailoring learning to the particular student and setting. The very richness of potential opportunities also necessitates some process for narrowing the choices, prioritizing the objectives, and specifying the tasks.

## POTENTIAL INCONGRUENCE WITH HUMANIST EDUCATION

Serious objections have been raised to using learning contracts. The primary target of such objections is most often the measurable behavioral objective. The long-standing controversy between "behaviorists" and "humanists" about the costs and benefits of using behavioral objectives for instruction goes to the very core of the nature of education.

This ongoing controversy is summarized well by David Pratt (1976), who attempted a synthesis of the seemingly polar positions. (For a thorough analysis by a behaviorist of the pros and cons of behavioral objectives, see MacDonald-Ross, 1973.) Pratt notes that behaviorists and humanists agree that education is an intentional process. However, behaviorists have taken this to mean that the objectives (intents) "should determine the content and direction of instruction." That is, behaviorists have maintained that, if education is intentional, then a teacher should be able to communicate unambiguously the purpose of the instructional unit. They argue that this is best done by stating instructional objectives in terms of the measurable behaviors or performances that would demonstrate mastery of the objectives. Behaviorists emphasize that writing instructional objectives in behavioral terms forces instructors to clarify what they actually want students to learn, assures a clear understanding of what is expected, and assures greater objectivity in the assessment of achievement. This position is usually associated with Ralph Tyler (1949, 1961), though there are antecedents among earlier educators. It was developed and popularized by educators such as Burns (1972), Bloom, Englehart, Furst, Hill, and Krathwohl (1956), Krathwohl, Bloom, and Masia (1964), Mager (1962, 1972), McAshan (1970, 1974), and Popham (1969, 1973). Pratt characterizes the behaviorist orientation as "action without reflection" (p. 17).

In contrast, humanists suggest that education does not result in a single, uniform, predetermined outcome that can be stated in behavioral terms. Rather, education is the provision of experience. The actual outcomes, the results of this experience expressed by different learners, vary widely, including different world views, new concepts of and resolutions to problems, challenges to established assumptions, art. Humanists argue that the most important features of education cannot be described in behavioral terms or measured. For the humanist, instruction involves the selection of "valuable experiences, the results of which may be multifarious but. . .presumably. . .beneficial. . ." (p. 18). Pratt characterizes the humanist orientation as "reflection without action" (p. 18).

But Pratt and other humanists, as well as educators who support the notion of writing instructional objectives, have pointed to a number of problems with the behaviorist orientation and with writing instructional objectives as measurable behavioral outcomes. In his effort to achieve a synthesis out of the controversy between humanists and behaviorists around the issue of instructional objectives, Pratt (1976) argues that a "behavioral objective," when applied to education and training, is a contradiction in terms because a behavior is a single action at a specific time, whereas the objectives of education and training are continuing states. Pratt advocates ending the "training-versus-education" controversy by acknowledging that both are necessary and important functions of schooling. He proposes a definition of training as "instruction which develops some permanent capability or state" and education as "the provision of significant or intrinsic experiences" (p. 23).

An understanding of this debate can lead to informed decisions, first, about whether to use learning contracts, and second, about what format and process minimizes or avoids potentially negative effects. We review, therefore, seven issues in the controversy.

## Nature of Education

The primary objection to behavioral objectives is that education is a complex endeavor that cannot be reduced to measurable behavioral objectives. Education is a personal change process. Change in behavior is part of the process, but not the entirety.

Some authors argue that the behaviorist orientation distorts the basic nature and aim of education. According to Jack Nelson (1976), "the primary goal of education is continuing human improvement and the means. . .is some form of critical inquiry" (p. 562). Nelson maintains that neither is measurable by behavioral observations alone.

> Human improvement sets a broad qualitative and ethical standard within which there is considerable latitude for discussion, debate and change. Critical inquiry requires information about things, skills in communication and computation, and competency in reasoned judgment, but it is more than the sum of these parts. It is a skeptical orientation, a willingness to consider the implausible, a manner of thought and action that is not completely explained by a long list of particular behaviors. The very looseness of these concepts, a part of their strength in encouraging diversity and individuality, is their most serious defect in behavioral terms because they are not subject to operational definitions and precise behavioral measurement without losing their essential quality. (p. 562)

Robert Leight (1979) makes a similar point, that education seeks to develop complex skills that cannot be behaviorally described. He discusses the specific constructs of "interpersonal relations" and "problem solving" as examples of the inadequacy of behavioral definitions: "these are complex operations, and operational definitions. . .cannot capture the subtlety of either" (p. 338). Leight points out that even though Dewey delineated a series of stages in the problem-solving process, he emphasized "the necessity of imagination and innovation." Leight concludes,

> my argument is that at the higher levels, problem solving activities deal with novel solutions, require great creativity, and cannot follow a prescribed path to a preordained answer. The true test of the problem solving process is the rigor of application and the ingenuity. . . .Although I am convinced that problem solving can be *taught*, I am just as thoroughly convinced that the capacity to solve problems cannot be specified in minimum terms and measured with confidence. . . .The very complexity of the process and the diversity of approaches which are possible will prove to be extremely frustrating to those who are charged with establishing minimum competencies in problem solving. (pp. 338-339)

Other authors argue that "we probably don't know or can't identify many of our most important educational objectives" (Shumate,

1974, p. 102). These educators point out that we do not know what combination of factors leads to creative thinking capacities, nor is it likely that there is a single process for all people.

The humanists acknowledge the validity of both intrinsic and incidential learning. Pratt (1976) points out that behaviorists assume all educational activity is instrumental, a means to an end. In contrast, humanists assume that much human activity, including education, is intrinsically valuable: activities are ends in themselves. Pratt's illustrations of intrinsically valuable activities include painting a picture, seeing a play, riding a horse, and wandering through the streets of Florence. Education, then, encompasses "experiential objectives," which are intrinsically valuable, objectives that may have desirable results but whose primary intent is to be "directly interesting, satisfying, enjoyable, etc." (p. 22).

A closely related issue, given much attention by both schools, is incidental learning, i.e., the unintended by-product of learning experiences that had other purposes. Incidental learning is an important element in the development of an "educated person." By definition, incidental learning cannot be specified in advance by objectives.

In social work education, for example, we cannot specify in advance all the kinds of learning that might contribute to developing the complex network of skills, knowledge, values, attitudes, and personal style that make an effective practitioner with a strong professional identity. This is not to say that we do not know many of the specifics that must be learned, only that we do not know the totality of what makes effective social workers nor all of the ways that people learn these things. This may be a failure of knowledge, but it is more likely, and probably fortunate, that human beings and social work roles are sufficiently complex and varied that there is no single answer.

One logical extension of using behavioral objectives is competency-based education — the design of entire programs so that successful completion (and thus preparation for a profession) can be measured via a set of behavioral outcomes. One problem with this approach is the assumption that there is or can be consensus about what the ideal competencies would be (setting aside, for the moment, the question of whether they could be taught and measured even if they could be specified). Westbury (1978) notes that "it is not clear that either social work or teacher education knows what competency in professional practice is. The parameters of practice in both of these professions are relatively uncodified; the means-ends linkages that make up successful practice are unclear and the criteria of successive intervention or transaction are elusive" (p. 155).

Diamonti and Murphy (1977) address the same issues. They note that a group of scholars advocating competency-based education for rehabilitation counselors "implied that there exists universal agreement regarding the roles and functions of the rehabilitation counselor. However, even a cursory examination of the literature. . .reveals that the proper role. . .has been an ongoing subject of controversy for many years" (p. 53).

## Confusion Between Indicators and Objectives

If education is a complex process, yet there is a desire to express the objectives of education in measurable terms, oversimplification is inevitable. For example, Pratt (1976) suggests that a behaviorist might write the following objective:

> The student will run 2,000 m in 10 minutes on level track or roadway, on a still sunny day, wearing appropriate running clothes, with his pulse returning to normal ± 10 within 10 minutes of completing the run. (p. 19)

Pratt notes that the real intent (objective) "is that the student be physically fit: running 2,000 m in 10 minutes is merely the indicator that fitness has been achieved" (p. 19). Of course this is only one of many indicators of physical fitness. Pratt observes that teachers often get caught up in writing behavioral objectives and forget the larger purpose for wanting the student to demonstrate certain specific skills. Consequently, Pratt urges that "objectives" be statements of broad capabilities, and that the term "performance criteria" be used to label the measurable outcomes that serve as sample indicators of the achievement of the objective. He also emphasizes that no small sample of behaviors can demonstrate the achievement of an objective, and that we should be aware of the imperfection of our measurement.

Similar critiques are made by Gronlund (1970) and Popham (1973). Gronlund criticizes instructional objectives that represent a "one-to-one relationship between the behavior taught and the behavior tested" (p. 5). He recommends writing "general instructional objectives" and then clarifying each objective by listing a sample of specific behaviors (or learning outcomes) that would be acceptable as evidence of the attainment of the objective. Popham makes a similar point in urging that objectives possess "content generality," that is, describe "a range of specific kinds of learner responses rather than a single test item" (p. 196).

On this very point both Popham and Gronlund are critical of Robert Mager's (1962) classic programmed text. Gronlund says that objectives such as those in Mager's book are "characteristic of the training level" and are useful only for teaching the simplest skills and the lowest level of knowledge" (p. 5). Popham observes, "despite the tremendous beneficial influences Bob Mager's book has had, there have been some deleterious side effects. The vast majority of Mager's examples tend to deal with rather low level instructional outcomes. There were some readers who erroneously assumed that a proponent of measurable instructional objectives had to, of necessity, endorse the most prosaic kinds of goals" (p. 192).

Other authors make a similar point about confusing indicators with objectives when they argue that the whole (the objective) is more than the sum of its parts (measurable indicators). Nelson (1976), in comments quoted earlier, argues that critical inquiry is something more than the sum of a list of discrete skills. In the same article, he observes:

> The basis of behavioral/competency objectives lies in the analysis, or breaking down, of large-scale behaviors into parts which can be physically observed and measured. . .A list of specific behaviors. . .presumably adds up to a whole. . . . This emphasis on analysis would be appropriate if teaching were only a technical skill, but the most important work of teaching may be in synthesizing bits of information and skills into something more artistic than technological. Science itself is more than analysis; in its best sense science strives for synthesis. (p. 563)

Similarly, Diamonti and Murphy (1977) suggest that

> a distinction must be made between knowing the component parts of a skill and the artful performance of the skill itself. . .one may be able to

successfully fulfill all the subroutines of bicycle riding — steering, pedaling, balancing correctly on a seat, etc. — yet the coherence of all these component parts into a working "gestalt" is not guaranteed. One may, in fact, not be able to put them all together and may fail miserably at riding a bicycle. This is a very real problem when applied to the area of professional training and practice. (p. 53)

The concern here is that designing education around behavioral objectives requires division of the comprehensive goal into smaller, measurable units, and in the process, significant aspects of education are lost.

A related point is made by Thomas and Ezell (1972) in their discussion of the contract as a technique for counseling high school students. They observe that if a student makes a contract to change specific behaviors, that student may "fulfill a contract without gaining any real insight into the causes of his original behavior or the reasons this (new) behavior is better" (p. 30). Applying this point to learning contracts, a student might fulfill all the specific requirements of the contract without understanding the purpose of the activities.

One final element of confusion between indicators and objectives is the distinction between learning behaviors and becoming educated. The objectives of education and training usually seek to develop *continuing states* or *ongoing capacities*. Since behaviors are actions limited in time, behavioral measures can only be *indicators* of the achievement of an educational or training objective. The performance of certain behaviors is not in itself the objective of education (Pratt, 1976, pp. 21-22).

## Reductionism and Quantification

A common criticism is that writing educational objectives in behavioral terms results in a "naive reductionism," a focus on the trivial, the superficial, the quantifiable. Armitage and Clark (1975) write, "The most feasible assessment is the most significant. That is, the emphasis on assessment. . .may focus attention on the easily assessible but trivial behavior" (p. 28). Naive reductionism is inevitable if the two pitfalls discussed above are not resolved, i.e., if the domain of education is limited only to learning that can be predetermined and stated in behavioral terms and if objectives are confused with indicators. Ivancevich, McMahon, Streidl, and Szilagyi (1978) note that one negative consequence of goal setting programs is "an overemphasis on production and productivity — on what is called the 'hard' performance indicators" (p. 61). This overemphasis tends to ignore or to minimize the amount of attention given other less measurable indicators of achievement.

Diamonti and Murphy (1977) suggest that much of the impetus for measurable educational outcomes has come from pressures for accountability and efficiency in using educational funds. Consequently, there is a need to demonstrate, in quantifiable terms, what an educational program has produced. They argue against simplifying education into "atomized behavioral elements" (p. 53).

Social work practitioners have seen the results of quantification in their jobs. The pressure for accountability has shifted concern from the quality of services provided to the numbers of contacts, the number of cases closed, et cetera. The quality of social work services is difficult to measure, so job performance and agency achievement is determined on the basis of less complex, and often less significant, indicators.

Similarly in education, there is the risk that behavioral objectives will focus on the quantifiable, that which is most easily measured, even though it may be less important. We may lose track of whether what we teach is worth learning. We may forget to ask the questions "What is an educated social worker?" and "What should social workers learn?" In Nelson's (1976) words, "There is an obvious danger that the least important aspects of teaching and learning become the most required simply because they are the easiest to measure" (p. 563).

Nelson also expresses concern that behavioral indicators tend to eliminate issues of quality. That is, the emphasis is on whether a person is able to perform a task, not on how well it is performed. "To remain objective a behavioral/competency program only measures the *existence* of a behavior, not its *quality*. How *well* a person performs a task is too subjective to measure" (p. 563, emphasis added). Thus behavioral measures are more likely to focus on how many times a behavior is performed or how many of a list of behaviors are performed rather than to focus on qualitative aspects of the performance. Many students have participated in classes where they could "contract" for a grade, and most frequently the criteria for each grade were the number and difficulty of assignments, not the quality of performance.

## Restricting Content of Course and Role of Instructor

This fourth danger emerges from the third. Emphasis on the behavioral and measurable may detrimentally shape the character and content of the course. If students are to be evaluated exclusively on measurable items, teachers will be under pressure — from students, administrators, and themselves — to focus on teaching students only what is measurable. Such a focus precludes exploration of broader issues, or any issues of interest not related directly to the measurable objectives.

In an article on the use of behavioral objectives in elementary school reading programs, Harriet Shenkman (1978) bemoans a shift in the function of teachers:

> The instructor becomes absorbed in measuring the selected skills, assigning exercises, remeasuring the same skills and keeping charts, graphs, and other records. S/he believes that his/her instructional duty has been satisfied once s/he has "covered" all the objectives and completed the record keeping procedures. In effect, the educational program becomes metamorphosed into a training system. (p. 114)

Similarly, when social agencies shift their emphasis to quantifiable information, social workers become "case managers" — workers responsible for seeing that a series of mechanical tasks are accomplished and reported within given time frames.

While college teaching is not likely to become this mechanized, the concern is nevertheless valid. There is danger that teachers will assist students in achieving a list of specified objectives rather than in developing crucial capacities.

In short, there is continual danger, especially in professional education, that teachers will become trainers rather than educators. Professional education requires elements of both training and education. No mechanism should push us toward one to the exclusion of the other.

## Rigidity and Conformity

A fifth concern is that objectives may lead to rigidity in the curriculum and the instruction, which would reinforce passivity, conformity, conservatism, arrogance, and a narrow view of the profession. These dangers are particularly of concern in a competency-based program where the competencies and the measures of their achievement have been specified in advance. Thus, rather than a *contract* developed through negotiation, faculty preselect content and students are rewarded for passively, uncritically absorbing it. Such a process not only violates the principles of progressive education and adult education discussed earlier in this chapter, but it also socializes the learners into the notion that "passivity and uncritical thought are important ingredients for success" in the professional world (Diamonti & Murphy, 1977, p. 53).

Nelson (1976) argues that competency-based education reinforces conservatism and arrogance, stresses adjustment rather than expansion, sacrifices creativity for conformity, and destroys professionalism while expanding fiscal conservatism. He notes that competencies are selected by the established, arrogant, elite powers in a profession and thus tend to reflect the orientation of the "gatekeepers" of tradition. The normal corrective to this general tendency in education is the loose structure and elasticity of most educational programs; but this tends to be diminished or lost when outcomes are made very specific and teachers' options are restricted by the design of a competency-based program. Consequently, students are expected to *adjust* to the norms of the majority rather than to *expand* their horizons, the historic conception of one of the central functions of education. Furthermore, since the competencies are established and specified, conformity to those competencies is expected and rewarded, and original, unusual, and spontaneous activity is discouraged. This whole process reinforces the idea that the tasks of the profession are appropriately shaped by concerns for accountability and efficiency rather than by a vision and a set of values held by the profession.

Potential for rigidity and loss of creativity also occurs at various stages of curriculum development and implementation. Atkin (in Shumate, 1974) warns that some innovations are likely to be hampered if behavioral statements are required too early, i.e., before the new idea has had time to mature. Similarly the options for curriculum developers may be limited if there are demands for immediate behavioral specification. Atkin also notes that focusing teacher attention on behavioral outcomes may divert attention from other important parts of the learning situation.

Another pitfall, discussed in a different context earlier, is that once competencies are formulated, programs become "fixed and rigid," with emphasis on the management aspects of teaching rather than on substantive issues (Shenkman, 1978, pp. 113-114).

While individual contracts are usually seen to encourage individualization and liberation, Seabury (1976) observes that if they are fixed, nonnegotiable, and strictly binding, they become tools of oppression, not tools of liberation. The contract can be used "as an excuse to apply strong negative sanctions" (p. 20) when persons do not meet the terms of the contract.

## Time and Assessment

Two other problems with learning contracts deserve mention. One is the practical reality, that contracts are individually constructed and negotiated instruments and thus require a tremendous amount of instructor time and energy. Consequently, there are constraints on the extent to which learning contracts can be used in educational programs (Colby, 1978). The other problem is that learning contracts tend to focus on the competencies of the student, sometimes to the exclusion of evaluating the skills of the instructor in facilitating the learning (Armitage & Clark, 1975; Bernstein & LaComte, 1976).

## RELATED RESEARCH FINDINGS

Little research has been done on the effects of learning contracts on learning outcomes, and for the most part what has been done has not used experimental design (for one notable exception, see Goldman, 1978). Rather, it has involved self-reports by participants in contract learning (Chickering, 1975; Lehmann, 1975) and/or subjective judgments of the teacher/researcher (Barlow, 1974).

On the other hand, there is a considerable volume of research on the effects of behavioral objectives on learning, the effects of goal setting on task performance, and the effects of participation in setting goals/objectives on performance. While a comprehensive review of the research literature is beyond the scope of this chapter, it is useful to call attention to relevant findings. (For reviews of this research literature, see Duchastel & Merrill, 1973; Latham & Yuhl, 1975; Melton, 1978.)

First, many studies support the finding that setting specific goals results in higher levels of performance than not setting goals or setting generalized goals of "doing the best you can." (See Gaa, 1973; Ivancevich & McMahon, 1977; Latham, Mitchell, & Dossett, 1978; Latham & Yuhl, 1975; Locke, 1968.) Other studies have not found higher performance as a result of goal setting (Duchastel & Merrill, 1973; Melton, 1978); these studies have not refuted the principle but have provided insights into the complexity of the interaction and the conditions that limit its operation (see p. 74).

Second, as long as the goals are accepted, the more difficult or challenging the goal, the higher the level of achievement (Becker, 1978; Latham et al., 1978; Latham & Yuhl, 1975; Locke, 1966a, 1967). One of the limiting conditions to this principle is that unrealistically high goals do not result in higher performance, apparently because they are seen as unattainable and thus are not accepted (Latham & Yuhl, 1975). Locke and Bryan (1967), however, found that "even when the empirical probability of reaching the harder goal was less than 10%, this goal produced higher output than did goals which were easier to achieve" (p. 120). Other studies indicate an interaction between educational attainment and the effects of goal difficulty on level of performance. Ivancevich and McMahon (1977) found that "Goal challenge was significantly related to performance for more educated technicians, while goal clarity and goal feedback were significantly related to performance for less educated technicians" (p. 92). They suggest that the more educated are motivated by challenging goals, while the less educated are motivated by clarity of expectations and feedback about progress.

Third, a series of studies has demonstrated "a linear relationship between degree of task success and degree of liking for and satisfaction with the task" (Locke, 1965, p. 384; see also, Locke, 1966b). This relationship does not hold in the case of extremely difficult goals: "the hardest goals lead to the lowest degree of satisfaction with, and liking for, the task" (Locke & Bryan, 1967, p. 129), even though the harder goals produce a higher level of achievement (Gaa, 1973, p. 23). Locke and Bryan note that since failure to reach goals makes subjects less likely to want to perform the tasks again, some compromise seems to be necessary "to achieve both high output and satisfaction" (p. 129).

Fourth, feedback regarding progress toward goals increases the level of performance (Becker, 1978), but only if the feedback is related to predetermined specific goals or results in increasing specificity of goals. The more specific the goals, the greater the results of the feedback (Latham et al., 1978). Performance feedback provides both motivation and learning. Having one's degree of success evaluated provides incentives to recognize the feasibility of achieving the predetermined goal or an even higher goal, and to work harder to achieve the goal. Feedback produces learning when it clarifies what is required to achieve the goal or problem-solves regarding more effective performance (Latham & Yuhl, 1975).

Fifth, the findings regarding participation in goal setting are surprising. Latham et al. (1978) conclude that participation does not lead to any greater *acceptance* of goals than does assignment of goals, as long as "the goals are realistic and are not based on whim or caprice" (p. 167). However, participation in goal setting leads to setting more difficult goals, and since more difficult goals lead to higher performance, participation in goal setting leads to higher performance. They also observe that even though persons who participated in goal setting generally set higher goals than the goals that were assigned by supervisors, "the *perceptions* of goal difficulty were not significantly different. . ." (p. 167, original emphasis). Gaa's (1973) research indicates that practice in goal setting leads to setting more realistic goals. There may be important connections, then, between participation, setting difficult yet realistic goals, and having a high degree of success and thus a high degree of satisfaction.

Finally, researchers have sought to determine the effects of behavioral objectives on learning directly related to those objectives and on incidental learning, that is, learning not specifically designated in the objectives. While those who advocate the use of behavioral objectives have claimed that it enhances "relevant learning," those opposed to behavioral objectives have argued that they "discourage students from expanding their horizons by encouraging them to confine their learning to specified objectives, and as a result incidental learning is depressed (Melton, 1978, p. 291). In summarizing research findings, Melton (1978) concludes that behavioral objectives *enhance relevant learning* except under certain conditions: (1) students ignore the objectives, either because they are unaware of them or because prior experience suggests they are unimportant; (2) the objectives are too general or ambiguous; (3) the objectives are too easy or too difficult; (4) the objectives of particular interest are only a small proportion of those provided; or (5) the students are so conscientious or so highly motivated that they achieve the objectives regardless of whether they are specified (p. 294). On the other hand, research findings generally agree that, since objectives are "expected to function as orienting stimuli" (p. 298), they narrowly focus the attention of the learner and thus tend to depress incidental learning.

## THE VALID CONTRACT: A RESOLUTION

An agreement or learning contract is inherent in all educational programs. When this agreement is *formal* rather than informal, *explicit* rather implicit, *individualized* rather than standardized, *mutual* and *reciprocal* rather than dictated and unilateral, *dynamic* rather than rigid, and *realistic* rather than utopian, learner and facilitator can together create a valid contract. In this concluding section, we present seven characteristics of a valid contract, several of which are drawn from the literature (see Adelman & Taylor, 1977; Maluccio & Marlow, 1974; Seabury, 1976). A valid contract, then, adheres to the principles of humanist and adult education and, through structure and process, resolves the dilemmas raised by the seven problems discussed in this chapter.

1. FORMALITY. Contracts are written documents that are matters of record for continual reference and use and that follow a specific format. We have developed a format, adapted from Gronlund (1970), that provides for goals, objectives, indicators, activities, and

evaluation processes. The format is presented in detail in the next chapter. It consists of goals, which are statements of broad, general, long-term purpose. The goals are *not* measurable behavioral objectives. They provide the rationale for the objectives and a basis for judging the appropriateness of the objectives.

The format also distinguishes between objectives and indicators. To use the Pratt (1976) illustration quoted earlier, the format makes it clear that "physical fitness" is the objective and that running a given distance in a given time with a resulting pulse rate is only an indicator of the achievement of the objective. Thus the objectives possess "content generality," that is, they describe "a range of specific kinds of learner responses rather than a single test item" (Popham, 1973, p. 195). The objectives represent continuing states, which Pratt says should be expressed by verbs such as know, understand, be, or enjoy. Each objective is clarified by a list of indicators, or what Pratt calls "performance criteria." Indicators are expressed in observable or measurable terms such as demonstrate, write, define, identify, distinguish between. A list of indicators is a *sample* of the specific behaviors that would be accepted as evidence of the attainment of the objective. Gronlund observes that it is impossible to list all the behaviors that might demonstrate the achievement of an objective, so "we must settle for a representative sample" of the types of behavior that describe the objective (1970, p. 5).

This format is more than a matter of literary form. It is a way to recognize the complexity of learning and the validity of intrinsic and incidental learning. It avoids reductionism and quantification. It provides for diversity and creativity in the objectives chosen and in the way one demonstrates achievement of those objectives — and thus takes into account individual differences in ways to learn and in ways to demonstrate learning. The clear distinction between objectives and indicators keeps both learner and facilitator focused on the purpose of the learning rather than only on performance of certain behaviors.

2. EXPLICITNESS. The provisions of contracts are throroughly delineated and clearly stated in specific, concrete terms. Such clarity facilitates subsequent evaluation of the performance of both learner and facilitator. Vague or ambiguous language may lead to misunderstandings, misdirected energies, and bad feelings. Whenever possi-

ble the agreement should indicate each expectation, how competence will be demonstrated, a timetable, and who is responsible for the prerequisite learning activities.

3. INDIVIDUALIZATION. Contracts provide a framework for designing a unique learning experience for each student. Within the constraints of the program and the learning opportunities, students can select those goals and objectives best suited to their special interests and abilities. They can design a unique set of learning experiences reflecting their developmental statuses and their personal learning styles. They can select ways to demonstrate their competencies that fit their own strengths. Maximizing learner input in the shaping of the learning contract assures a highly motivated learner who sees and feels the relevance of the educational experience.

4. MUTUALITY. Contracts reflect the goals and tasks students anticipate for themselves. They also reflect faculty choices based on program intent and instructor assessment of student experience, knowledge, skills, and values. Since contracts are mutual agreements, developing learning contracts requires explanation, persuasion, and negotiation. Ideally, the final product will reflect the best thinking of the negotiators — persons who bring different perspectives, knowledge, experience, and insights to building the contract. The document represents a compromise, but the process of developing the contract should assure full understanding, endorsement, and commitment by all parties.

5. RECIPROCITY. Contracts are created through collaboration and implemented through reciprocal, although differential, participation and responsibility. The specified objectives and activities squarely place the major responsibility for their own learning on students. For the endeavor to succeed, however, complementary responsibilities must be fulfilled. The faculty must provide liaison and instruction; the agency must provide learning opportunities and instruction. Regular occasions for evaluation should be provided in the contract. The evaluations assess the performance and progress of the learner as well as the adequacy of learning opportunities and instruction.

6. DYNAMISM. To be truly responsive to the growing sophistication and abilities of the student, as well as to changes in the learning environment, the contract must be reviewed and renegotiated pe-

riodically. Learning contracts presuppose change and carry no penalty for renegotiation. They "are not written to be a priori rules to cover all contingencies nor are they expected to be followed blindly" (Seabury, 1976, p. 17). They are, however, mutual covenants and thus cannot be ignored, circumvented, or modified at the whim of one party. Just as the original contract was mutually agreed upon so also must modifications be subject to negotiation and mutual consent. As changes occur in the learning environment or in the vision of what is possible or desired, discussions, renegotiations, and modifications of the contract are advisable. These changes may require deleting parts of the contract no longer feasible, adding opportunities, or reformulating or further specifying objectives.

7. REALISM. Learning contracts must set terms that are within the capacity of students and achievable given the available resources. Faculty time and expertise must be considered. The constraints under which host agencies operate inevitably limit learning opportunities. Similarly, a college or community can only provide the resources at its disposal. These resources often must be allocated to more than one student. Unrealistic provisions, no matter how desirable and well intended, can only lead to failure and frustration. If a learning contract is to extend boundaries of knowledge, values, and skill, it must challenge, but it must also succeed.

## REFERENCES

Adelman, H., & Taylor, L. Two steps toward improving learning for students with (and without) "learning problems." *Journal of Learning Disabilities,* 1977, *10,* 66-72.

Armitage, A., & Clark, F.W. Design issues in the performance-based curriculum. *Journal of Education for Social Work,* 1975, *11*(1), 22-29.

Barlow, R.M. An experiment with learning contracts. *Journal of Higher Education,* 1974, *45,* 441-449.

Becker, L.J. Joint effect of feedback and goal setting on performance: A field study of residential energy conservation. *Journal of Applied Psychology,* 1978, *63,* 428-433.

Bernstein, B.L., & LaComte, C. An integrative competency-based counselor education model. *Counselor Education and Supervision,* 1976, *16,* 26-36.

Berte, R. (Ed.). *Individualizing education through contract learning.* University, AL:

University of Alabama Press, 1975.

Bigge, M.L. *Learning theories for teachers.* New York: Harper & Row, 1964.

Bloom, B.S., Englehart, M.D., Furst, E.J., Hill, W.H., & Krathwohl, D.R. (Eds.). *A taxonomy of educational objectives: Handbook I, the cognitive domain.* New York: David McKay, 1956.

Brigham, T.M. Liberation in social work education: Applications from Paulo Freire. *Journal of Education for Social Work,* 1977, *13*(3), 5-11.

Bruner, J.S. *Toward a theory of instruction.* Cambridge, MA: Belknap Press, 1966.

Burns, R.W. *New approaches to behavioral objectives.* Dubuque, IA: W.C. Brown Co. Publishers, 1972.

Chickering, A. Developing intellectual competence at Empire State. In N. Berte (Ed.), *Individualizing education through contract learning.* University, AL: University of Alabama Press, 1975.

Cleghorn, J.M., & Levin, S. Training family therapists by setting learning objectives. *American Journal of Orthopsychiatry,* 1973 *43,* 439-446.

Colby, I.C. Contract grading: An assessment technique for social work education. *Journal of Social Welfare,* 1978, *5*(2), 19-24.

Coles, R. *Children of crisis.* Boston: Little, Brown, 1967.

Diamonti, M.C., & Murphy, S.T. Behavioral objectives and rehabilitation counseling education: A critique. *Rehabilitation Counseling Bulletin,* 1977, *21,* 51-66.

Dewey, J. *Democracy and education.* New York: Free Press, 1916.

Dewey, J. *Art as experience.* New York: Minton, Balch & Co., 1934.

Duchastel, P.C., & Merrill, P.F. The effects of behavioral objectives on learning: A review of empirical studies. *Review of Educational Research,* 1973, *43,* 53-70.

Flanigan, B. Planned change and contract negotiation as an intructional model. *Journal of Education for Social Work,* 1974, *10*(2), 34-39.

Freire, P. *Pedogogy of the oppressed.* New York: Seabury Press, 1970.

Gaa, J.P. Effects of individual goal-setting conferences on achievement, attitudes, and goal setting behavior. *The Journal of Experimental Education,* 1973, *42,* 22-28.

Gilbert, J. Contract learning. *Alternative Higher Education,* 1976, *1,* 25-32.

Goodman, P. *Growing up absurd.* New York: Random House, 1962.

Gronlund, N.E. *Stating behavioral objectives for classroom instruction.* New York: Macmillan, 1970.

Goldman, G. Contract teaching of academic skills. *Journal of Counseling Psychology,* 1978, *25,* 320-324.

Hartwig, J.E. A competency-based approach to adult counseling and guidance. *Counselor Education and Supervision,* 1975, *15,* 12-20.

Hilgard, E.R., & Bower G.H. *Theories of learning* (3rd ed.). New York: Appleton-Century-Crofts, 1966.

Hokenstad, M.C., & Rigby, B.D. *Participation in teaching and learning: An idea book for social work educators.* New York: International Association of Schools of Social Work, 1977.

Holt, J.C. *How children fail.* New York: Pitman, 1964.

Holt, J.C. *Underachieving school.* New York: Pitman, 1969.

Houpt, J.L., Weinstein, H.M., & Russell, M.L. The application of competency-based education to consultation-liaison psychiatry. *International Journal of Psychiatry in Medicine,* 1977, *7,* 295-320.

Illich, I. *De-schooling society.* New York: Harper & Row, 1971.

Ivancevich, J.M., & McMahon, J.T. Education as a moderator of goal setting effectiveness. *Journal of Vocational Behavior,* 1977, *11,* 83-94.

Ivancevich, J.M., McMahon, J.T., Streidl, J.W., & Szilagyi, A.D., Jr. Goal setting: The Tenneco approach to personnel development and management effectiveness. *Organizational Dynamics,* 1978, *6,* 58-80.

Kozol, J. *Death at an early age.* Boston: Houghton Mifflin, 1967.

Kozol, J. *Free schools.* Boston: Houghton Mifflin, 1972.

Knowles, M.S. *The modern practice of adult education: Andragogy versus pedagogy.* New York: Association Press, 1970.

Knowles, M.S. Innovations in teaching styles and approaches based upon adult learning. *Journal of Education for Social Work,* 1972, 8(2), 32-39.

Krathwohl, D.R., Bloom, B.S., & Masia, B. *A taxonomy of educational objectives: Handbook II, the affective domain.* New York: David McKay, 1964.

Latham, G.P., Mitchell, T.R., & Dossett, D. Importance of participative goal setting and anticipated rewards on goal difficulty and job performance. *Journal of Applied Psychology,* 1978, *63,* 163-171.

Latham, G.P., & Yuhl, G.A. A review of research on the application of goal setting in organizations. *Academy of Management Journal,* 1975, *18,* 824-845.

Lehmann, T. *Educational outcomes from contract learning at Empire State College,* 1975. (ERIC Document Reproduction Service No. ED 111 306)

Leight, R.L. Political goals as educational goals. *The Educational Forum,* 1979, *43,* 331-343.

Locke, E.A. The relationship of task success to task liking and satisfaction. *Journal of Applied Psychology,* 1965, *49,* 379-385.

Locke, E.A. The relationship of intentions to level of performance. *Journal of Applied Psychology,* 1966, *50,* 60-66. (a)

Locke, E.A. Relationship of task success to task liking: A replication. *Psychological Reports,* 1966, *18,* 522-524. (b)

Locke, E.A. Relationship of goal level to performance level. *Psychological Reports,* 1967, *20,* 1068.

Locke, E.A. Toward a theory of task motivation and incentives. *Organizational Behavior and Human Performance,* 1968, *3,* 157-189.

Locke, E.A., & Bryan, J. Performance goals as determinants of level of performance and boredom. *Journal of Applied Psychology,* 1967, *51,* 120-130.

MacDonald-Ross, M. Behavioral objectives — A critical review. *Instructional Science,* 1973, *2,* 1-52.

Mager, R.F. *Preparing instructional objectives.* Belmont, CA: Fearon Publishers, 1962.

Mager, R.F. *Goal analysis.* Belmont, CA: Fearon Publishers, 1972.

Maluccio, A.N., & Marlow, W.D. The case for the contract. *Social Work,* 1974,

*19,* 28-34.

McAshan, H.H. *Writing behavioral objectives: A new approach.* New York: Harper and Row, 1970.

McAshan, H.H. *The goals approach to performance objectives.* Philadelphia: W.B. Saunders Co., 1974.

Melton, R.F. Resolution of conflicting claims concerning the effect of behavioral objectives on student learning. *Review of Educational Research,* 1978, *48,* 291-302.

Nelson, J.L. A criticism of competency-based teacher education and behavioral objectives. *Social Education,* 1976, *40,* 561-563.

Popham, W.J. Objectives and instruction. In W.J. Popham, E. Eisner, H. Sullivan, & L. Tyler (Eds.), *Instructional objectives.* Chicago: Rand McNally, 1969.

Popham, W.J. Instructional objectives 1960-1970. *Improving Human Performance: A Research Quarterly,* 1973, *3,* 191-198.

Pratt, D. Humanistic goals and behavioral objectives: Toward a synthesis. *Journal of Curriculum Studies,* 1976, *8,* 15-25.

Seabury, B.A. The contract: Uses, abuses and limitations. *Social Work,* 1976, *21,* 16-21.

Shenkman, H. Beyond behavioral objectives: Behavioral processes. *Journal of Reading,* 1978, *22,* 113-116.

Shumate, N.M. Writing behavioral objectives. *Peabody Journal of Education,* 1974, *51,* 101-106.

Sommers, M.L. Contributions of learning and teaching theories to the explication of the role of the teacher in social work education. *Journal of Education for Social Work,* 1969, *5*(2), 61-73.

Sommers, M.L. Dimensions and dynamics of engaging the learner. *Journal of Education for Social Work,* 1971, *7*(3), 49-57.

Thomas, G.P., & Ezell, B. The contract as a counseling technique. *Personnel and Guidance Journal,* 1972, *51,* 27-31.

Tyler, R. *Basic principles of curriculum and instruction.* Chicago: University of Chicago Press, 1949.

Tyler, R.W. *Building the social work curriculum.* New York: Council on Social Work Education, 1961.

Westbury, I. Review of competency-based education for social work: Evaluation and curriculum issues. By M.L. Arkava, & E.C. Brennan (New York: CSWE, 1976), *Social Service Review,* 1978, *52,* 153-156.

# Chapter 4

# WRITING THE LEARNING CONTRACT

T HE previous chapter discussed the rationale for learning contracts, the benefits derived from their use, and the issues and problems that must be considered if the contracts are to be consistent with humanist education. This chapter is a guide for students, field instructors, and faculty coordinators who are or will be involved in developing social work field education learning contracts.

The chapter begins by defining the components and describing the content of learning contracts. This is followed by detailed explanations of goals, objectives, indicators, learning activities, and evaluation plans. Examples and practice exercises are included to let you test your understanding of the concepts and processes involved and to serve as a rehearsal for writing the contract that will shape your field education. It is a chapter to *do,* not just to read. Whenever a self-testing opportunity is provided, choose between the alternatives presented or fill in the blanks as requested before you continue reading.

## DEFINITIONS

To review, a learning contract is an agreement, collaboratively designed by student, field instructor, and faculty coordinator, that specifies intended educational outcomes, teaching/learning resources and methods, and evaluation processes. The format we recommend for field education contracts has the following elements:

1. *Goals* describe broad, long-term, nonmeasurable purposes, stated as outcomes, for undertaking a course of action.
2. *Learning objectives* describe discrete capabilities or states that are necessary but not sufficient for achieving the goal. They are,

81

in essence, subelements of the goal, and thus, even though stated as outcomes, they represent steps toward (or means and methods of achieving) the goal.

3. *Indicators* describe specific observable behaviors (performances) that give evidence of capabilities.
4. *Learning activities* describe all those experiences and tasks undertaken (thus the process/method used) to acquire the capabilities necessary to the goal.
5. *Evaluation plans* specify procedures and criteria for assessment.

As discussed in the previous chapter, a valid learning contract must have seven characteristics: formality (we recommend the format above), explicitness, individualization, mutuality, reciprocity, dynamism, and realism. The validity of the contract is determined both by the structure of the contract and by the process by which it is developed and utilized.

## CONTENT

There are various ways of selecting the content covered in learning contracts for social work education. We present five central dimensions of social work education that should be included in the contract for the field instruction segment of the curriculum. While a valid learning contract is by definition renegotiable, it is most useful if the original document is thorough, covering all dimensions of the curriculum as well as the individual wishes and needs of the learner.

1. SEQUENCES. Samuel Finestone (1969) argues that field education should be characterized by "a range of content that reflects the total social work curriculum" (p. 71). He emphasizes inclusion of content related to the four core sequences in social work education — human behavior in the social environment, social policy, research, and practice. Following this perspective, it is important to write learning objectives and activities related to all four sequences.

2. KNOWLEDGE, SKILLS, AND VALUES/ATTITUDES. The social work curriculum has traditionally acknowledged three aspects of education for the profession — knowledge, skills, and values/attitudes. The field education segment of the curriculum is more than a work experience or an apprenticeship focusing exclusively on

skill development. It is an *educational* endeavor integrating all three aspects. Thus the contract should give attention to theory and values as well as practice and provide time for study and reflection as well as action.

3. DIVERSITY. Social work education promotes understanding of factors causing alienation from society and develops competencies for working with alienated persons and groups. Therefore, the contract should include objectives for work with persons representing diversities such as race, ethnicity, gender, age, sexual preference, handicapping conditions, and socioeconomic status. Since work with diverse populations requires self-awareness, objectives are needed related to the ability to critique one's own values, attitudes, and skills and to recognize how these affect interactions with various people.

4. ROLES. Social work practice is often conceptualized in terms of roles. Though various authors have developed different typologies, the five most commonly identified roles are broker, enabler, teacher, mediator, and advocate. The skill clusters that make up these roles are generic to all social work practice. Each of the roles can be enacted at any system level, in any traditional practice method, and in any field of practice or social problem focus. Thus the learning contract should include all of these roles.

5. SPECIALIZATION. The contract should reflect the kind of practice for which the curriculum intends to prepare students. This may be generic practice, specialization in a field of practice (e.g., mental health or corrections), specialization in intervention at a given system level (e.g., micro or macro), specialization in a traditional practice method (e.g., casework or community organization), focus on a specific social problem (e.g., criminal justice or poverty), or a combination of these.

How can one learning contract cover all these content areas adequately? And does this list suggest a predetermined contract rather than the individualization discussed in the preceding chapter? It is true that the contract will need a number of objectives to reflect the full scope of social work education. However, several content areas may readily be combined into one objective. For example, writing an objective for learning the mediator role minimally requires specifying a sequence (practice) and certain component skills. Depending on the placement setting and the particular interests of the student, the same objective might also provide for diversity and values clarification. Individualization is also realized through the different amounts of time and energy assigned the chosen objectives, depending on the relative emphasis each student places on the various content areas.

## WRITING GOALS

Goals specify broad, long-term, nonmeasurable purposes for undertaking a course of action. Goals describe desired outcomes, or what one wants to achieve. Goals are reached through a set of prerequisite accomplishments called objectives. Objectives are also stated as outcomes, because they are ends in themselves as well as *means* to the ultimate end, the goal. As learners focus on achieving specific objectives, they may begin to see the objectives only as ends in themselves instead of steps toward the achievement of a larger intent. Goals, then, provide rationale for, and continual reminders of, the long-range intent for a variety of more specific objectives.

Goals also provide a basis for selecting and evaluating objectives. Seldom is there a single means to reach a goal. When choosing or assessing objectives, certain questions can be usefully asked. What are all the possible and appropriate objectives? Will the objectives that have been selected achieve the goal? Are there alternative objectives that would accomplish the same end? Are there additional objectives essential to achieving the goal?

The distinction between goals (the broad, long-term purposes) and objectives (the means to achieving the goal) is illustrated by the following exchange.

One social work student asks another, "Why are you in school?" and receives the answer, "I want a social work degree."

Is the degree the goal? Is it the broad, long-term purpose of going to school? To find out, the students might pursue the issue.

"Why do you want a social work degree?"

"The way our economy is going, I think social work is going to be one of the few places there will be jobs, and I want to be sure to have good, stable employment."

The same question might be asked of the other student.

"Why are you getting a social work degree?"

This time the answer might be,

"I'm concerned about the future of children in our society. I want to have the knowledge, skills and credentials essential to influencing legislation and policies related to children."

The social work degree, then, is not the goal for either of these students. In both cases, the degree is an objective, a sub-element of the goal. The degree is both an end in itself and a means to a larger goal. For one student the goal is the security of "good, stable employment." For the other it is children's welfare. Thus, the same objective can be the means to different goals. The goal specifies the purpose for accomplishing the objective.

Knowing the goal is absolutely essential to choosing the most effective means. Knowing the destination is crucial to choosing the best route. For example, there may be alternatives other than a social work degree for achieving the goals. The second student might seek a law degree or run for political office. The first student might take training in accounting, computers, or a building trade. In other words, there are alternative degree programs to achieve both goals, and there are also alternatives that do not require a college degree.

To return to the basic point, goal statements are the top of a hierarchy of statements of intent. They are statements expressing the most general, broad purpose. Next in the hierarchy are objectives and then indicators. Figure 1 illustrates the various levels of specificity of the educational intents of learning contracts. Three objectives (one knowledge, one value, and one skill) are listed under the goal, but additional objectives would be needed to represent the full achievement of the goal.

What are appropriate goals for field education learning contracts? The overriding goal of a social work program is to produce effective social workers whose practice reflects the values as well as the knowledge and skills that define the profession. Field education, as only one component of a total curriculum,

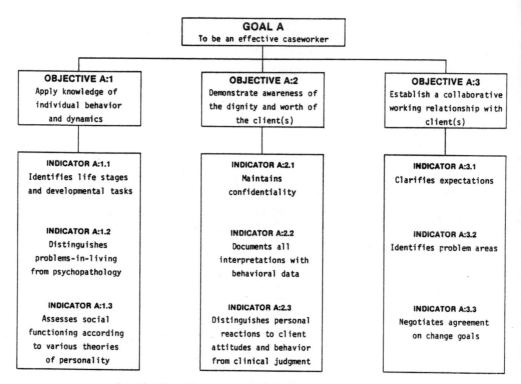

Note that the objectives represent knowledge, values, and skills respectively. Goals may have any number of objectives and indicators. This chart provides one example in each category.

Figure 1.

cannot by itself fulfill this comprehensive goal. Since field education occurs in a specific setting (even if the setting is a teaching/learning center rather than a single agency), goals are limited by what that setting can provide. Goals are also determined by the conceptualization of practice around which a particular social work program organizes its curriculum. The following are common formulations for organizing the curriculum:

*methods of practice,* e.g., casework-therapist, group work, supervision, community organization, planning, administration, research, teaching, generalist practice;

*intervention at different social system levels,* e.g., micro, mezzo, macro;

*fields of practice (practice settings),* e.g., aging, mental health, health, corrections, rural communities, developmental disabilities, child welfare; and

*social problem areas,* e.g., racism, poverty, crime, domestic violence.

Our purpose in this section is to enable you to distinguish between goals and objectives and then to write goals. Since both goals and objectives are stated as outcomes, the primary distinction is that the goal specifies the ultimate end of a change effort and the objectives the intermediate ends — which are also the means to the ultimate end.

Read the paired statements that follow and *circle* the one in each pair that is the broader statement of purpose:

1. To be an effective mediator with families.
2. To be an effective caseworker.
3. To be an effective medical social worker.
4. To be an effective discharge planner.
5. To be an effective social worker in Chicano communities.
6. To be an effective enabler with a Chicano group.

The second, third, and fifth statements are the goals, the broader statements of purpose. The first, fourth, and sixth are objectives, elements prerequisite to achieving the goals. As in the example of the two students, one of the ways to check the level of intent is to ask the question "why?" of any outcome statement.

The first pair of statements represents a social work curriculum organized around methods of practice. The mediator role would be seen as an essential component of the casework method. Thus, if the question were asked —

"Why do you want to be a mediator?"
a logical response would be —

"Because mediation is often essential to effective casework."

The second set of statements represents a curriculum organized around fields of practice. Discharge planning is one, but only one, function performed by medical social workers. Thus, if the question were asked —

"Why do you want to be able to do discharge planning?"
a logical response would be —

"Because arranging for posthospital care is integral to medical social work."

The third set of statements represents a curriculum organized around social problem areas. Enabling is only one of the skills the worker would put at the service of the Chicano community. Thus, if the question were asked —

"Why do you want to be an enabler with a Chicano group?"
a logical answer would be —

"Because enabling is crucial for social work with communities seeking empowerment."

Thus asking "why?" is a way to move up the hierarchy of levels of intent until you reach the level of a goal. Of course, you could pursue the question of purpose until you addressed global questions of the mission of social work, such as "facilitating personal and social change" or "improving the quality of life." An appropriate goal for social work education, and for field education as a component, is to prepare people to carry out that mission. Thus, once you reach the level where you are describing a professional identity, you have a statement comprehensive enough to provide a goal for your field education. You have reached the top level of the hierarchy of intent for a field education learning contract. Once your goal is clear, you can select the objectives prerequisite to reaching that goal.

Note that we used the phrase "to be an effective. . ." in all the paired statements. The phrase is one way of describing a "continuing state" and a professional identity. Other phrases may be equally descriptive, but we have found this one useful for goal-level statements. In the exercise, we used the phrase in both goal-level and objective-level statements. As you will see later, we suggest another terminology for objectives. We used the same lead-in phrase to help you discriminate between goals and objectives on the basis of content rather than phrasing, and to demonstrate that any outcome statement can be written in goal phrasing, even if it is not a goal-level statement.

Test yourself again. In the list below, circle the outcome statements that are goals.
1. To be an effective grant writer.
2. To be an effective supervisor of clinical services.
3. To be an effective case manager.
4. To be an effective social planner.
5. To be an effective industrial social worker.

The second, fourth, and fifth are goal statements. They are statements representing major social work identities used in the common formulations for organizing the curriculum: social planning and supervision are two methods of practice, and industrial social work is a field of practice. Some people may not consider "supervision of counseling services" a method of practice and may suggest that supervision is a component of administration. Our justification for identifying it as a goal is that, while supervision *is* a subelement of administration for an agency executive, we identified a specific function, "supervision of counseling services," which is often a primary identity in social work distinct from the agency administrator/executive role.

The first and third statements are not goals. Practice goal writing by identifying the goals for which these two statements are subelements. First, ask yourself, "Why would I want to be able to write grants?" and record the answer in the space below. Then continue asking the "Why?" question and recording the answers until you have identified the goal.

_____

_____

_____

_____

Now go through the same process with the third outcome statement above:

Why would you want "to be an effective case manager"?

_____

_____

_____

_____

As you attempted to go up the hierarchy of intent, starting with grant-writing skills, you probably decided that grant writing is one important part of fund raising, and then that fund raising is a major component of being an effective administrator or organizer. Even though it is true that some persons have full-time positions as grant writers, their practice is conceptualized within a larger social work identity. Similarly, case management is one subordinate skill of casework.

To review, the two basic principles to remember in writing field education learning goals are —

1. Field education goals are broad, long-term, nonmeasurable statements of purpose that refer to primary social work identities.
2. Field education goals are stated as outcomes (products, results) that describe continuing capabilities or states.

## WRITING OBJECTIVES AND INDICATORS

Objectives describe discrete capabilities or states that are necessary but not sufficient for achieving the goal. Thus they are ends in themselves (and consequently stated as outcomes), but they are also means or methods of achieving the goal.

As explained in Chapter 3, we have developed a format based on Gronlund (1970). Gronlund suggests that objectives should describe "learning *outcomes* toward which the student should be directed" (p. 8). They should be "specific enough to provide direction for instruction without overly restricting the teacher or reducing the instruction to the training level" (p. 10). Gronlund suggests verbs such as knows, understands, analyzes, comprehends, appreciates, applies, demonstrates, performs, uses. Objectives, then, possess what Popham (1973) calls "content generality," that is, they describe "a range of specific kinds of learner responses rather than a single test item" (p. 195)

Each objective is then defined and clarified by a list of *specific, observable behaviors* (performances) which we call *indicators*. Indicators are a *sample* of the terminal behaviors students are to demonstrate as evidence of the attainment of the objective. Gronlund suggests that indicators should begin with behavioral verbs such as defines, identifies, distinguishes between, recalls, interprets, constructs, prepares, lists, explains, relates, specifies. Indicators are what Pratt (1976) calls "performance criteria," that is, behaviors (performances) that serve as criteria determining whether the objective has been achieved. Since it would be impossible to list all the behaviors that might demonstrate the attainment of the objective, indicators only provide a representative sample of the types of behavior that describe the objective.

An example from Gronlund's book clarifies the content of objectives and indicators and the relationship between them:

1.  Understands the meaning of technical terms.
    1.1.  Defines the term in his own words.
    1.2.  Identifies the meaning of the term when used in context.
    1.3.  Distinguishes between terms that are similar in meaning. (p.4)

Gronlund emphasizes that this format is "more than a matter of literary form. This procedure makes clear that the instructional objective is *understanding* and not *defining, identifying,* or *distinguishing between.* . . .(The) sample of specific types of behavior. . .characterize(s) what is meant by the statement *understands the meaning of technical terms*". (p. 5, original emphasis).

Test your ability to identify objectives and indicators. Place an O (objective) or I (indicator) before each statement.

_____ 1.  Identifies the central issues on various sides of a policy controversy.

_____ 2.  Distinguishes between the constraints imposed by present laws and policies and the objectives of service to consumers.

_____ 3.  Gives leadership to management staff in clarifying issues and formulating policies.

_____ 4.  Formulates a draft policy for consideration by the management team.

You are correct if you identified the first, second, and fourth statements as indicators. Note that all of them refer to observable behaviors — behaviors that can be seen and verified by an outside observer. In contrast to the others, the third statement is at a higher level of generality; "giving leadership" is a complex concept representing a combination of several specific behaviors.

Note that objectives and indicators start with active verbs. Many authors recommend that all outcome statements start with infinitives — to identify, to distinguish, to lead, to formulate. This is another viable option. But Gronlund (1970) urges brevity and avoiding unnecessary words such as "to be able to," or "students should demonstrate that they can." We have adopted Gronlund's format for writing objectives and indicators and have reserved the infinitive form for writing goals.

Try another example to assure that you can distinguish learning objectives from indicators. Again, place an 0 (objective) or I (indicator) before each statement.

\_\_\_\_\_ 1. Describes the effect of each family member's behavior on the family group.

\_\_\_\_\_ 2. Assesses family functioning using a systemic perspective.

\_\_\_\_\_ 3. Identifies functional and dysfunctional communication patterns in families.

\_\_\_\_\_ 4. Specifies implicit rules of behavior in the family.

You should not have had any difficulty in identifying the second statement as an objective and the other three as indicators of that objective. Assessing family functioning is a general objective. Describing effects of behavior, identifying patterns, and specifying implicit rules are more specific, observable outcomes that give evidence of the ability to assess family functioning.

Another important principle in writing objectives is that they should be stated as learning outcomes, not processes. Objectives are not descriptions of the process of change occurring in the student but statements of the product or result.

The following exercise tests your grasp of the distinction between outcomes and processes. Before each sample statement place an 0 if it is an *outcome* statement or a P if it is a *process* statement.

_____ 1. Increases understanding of the social service system in the field of mental health.

_____ 2. Evaluates the quality of agency services.

_____ 3. Acquires skills in counseling.

_____ 4. Understands the nature and function of the judicial system.

You are correct if you identified the second and fourth items as outcome statements. They state the knowledge or skill that the student is expected to have at the conclusion of the contract period. The first and third items emphasize the *process* of the change. Words such as increases, acquires, gains, develops, and learns to, describe the learning process rather than the outcome that is expected at the end of the instruction period. Process statements refer to what the student is supposed to do *during* the teaching-learning experience but do not clarify what the student is supposed to be able to demonstrate as the *end product* of the instruction. If the outcome were to be some "increase" in knowledge and skills, the instructor would have to measure the beginning and ending points in order to know whether there has been an increase.

Now test your skills in actually writing an objective. The following is a list of indicators. In the space above the indicators, write an objective for which those indicators would demonstrate achievement.

1. _____

    1.1 Identifies neighborhood issues that residents consider problematic.

    1.2 Helps residents identify possible solutions.

    1.3 Mobilizes residents to attend planning meetings.

    1.4 Researches power relationships to determine the most effective intervention point.

Most likely you wrote an objective that said something like, "Organizes neighborhood residents to solve a problem that negatively affects their community." Organizing residents is a general objective that is demonstrated by the series of indicators listed.

Now reverse the process. The following is a general objective. Your task is to write indicators for the objective.

2. Works effectively with minority clientele and colleagues.

2.1 _____

_____

2.2 _____

_____

2.3 _____

_____

2.4 _____

_____

There are, of course, many different indicators you might have written. Some examples follow. Check your indicators against these examples, both for content and for format.

2.1 Describes sources of bias within self.

2.2 Distinguishes typical and functional cultural patterns from dysfunctional interpersonal behavior patterns.

2.3 Comprehends communication expressed in accents or dialects.

2.4 Recognizes culturally valued social roles and beliefs.

2.5 Advocates actions consistent with affirmative action principles.

2.6 Identifies social policies and institutional practices that affect minority clients negatively.

Note that each indicator begins with an active verb and describes an observable behavior that is fairly specific. As we have suggested previously, these are *sample* indicators. It is virtually impossible to list all of the potential indicators. You may have written an entirely different set of statements that are equally valid indicators of the achievement of the objective. The important issue is whether the content is appropriately related to the objective and whether the format, the way it is written, assures that it describes a *specific, observable behavior,* i.e., whether it describes an *outcome* in terms of an observable *performance*. It should also be noted that when the field instructor and student jointly select indicators, the groups of indicators written as a sample clarify for both what is meant by the objective and what aspects of that meaning are most important.

Here is another exercise to review how objectives and indicators are written and to check on your grasp of the principles involved. Following are two sets of objectives and indicators. In the spaces provided to the right of each statement, write "OK" if the statement is correct as written; if it is not correct as written, use the space to rewrite the statement in a way that corrects the problems you have identified. After each set we provide feedback and discussion.

1.  Protects patient rights (in medical setting)  _____

    1.1 Reads a book on patient rights  _____

    1.2 Believes in maintaining confidentiality — that records should be kept in locked files and that information should not be shared unnecessarily or inappropriately with colleagues.  _____

    1.3 Obtains signed release of information forms prior to consultations.  _____

    1.4 Learns about the principles and processes of informed consent.  _____

    1.5 Informs patients about possible eligibility for financial benefits.  _____

On the following page are our suggestions for improving the wording of this objective and set of indicators.

| | |
|---|---|
| 1. Protects patient rights (in medical setting) | OK |
|     1.1 Reads a book on patient rights | Lists and explains major patient rights. |
|     1.2 Believes in maintaining confidentiality — that records should be kept in locked files and that information should not be shared unnecessarily or inappropriately with colleagues. | Maintains confidentiality — keeps records in locked files and does not share information unnecessarily or without consent. |
|     1.3 Obtains signed release of information forms prior to consultations. | OK |
|     1.4 Learns about the principles and processes of informed consent. | Advocates for full understanding by patients before consent is asked or given — e.g., requests clear policy statement, questions persons who neglect this practice, urges patient to insist on it. |
|     1.5 Informs patients about possible eligibility for financial benefits. | OK |

The objective, "protects patient rights," is correctly stated. It describes a general outcome that must be subdivided into a number of specific, observable behaviors.

The first indicator is not stated as an outcome. It describes an *activity* or a learning *process*. That is, while it describes a very specific thing that you intend to *do*, it does not tell us what the result of that activity (or learning process) is supposed to be. If you recognized this flaw, you may have substituted one of several possible outcomes. The one we wrote suggests that the reason for reading the book was to know (have information about) what patient rights are — and so we wrote an indicator that represents a behavioral demonstration of that knowledge, namely "lists and explains major patient rights." You might have decided that the intended outcome was to write a paper, to give a speech, or to differentiate between patient and family rights. The important point is that your revision should have changed the statement from an activity, a learning process, to a specific, observable behavior that gives evidence of the outcome you intended to achieve.

The second statement, "believes in maintaining confidentiality . . .," is *too general* for an indicator. It is not stated in observable terms. If you "believe in" something, that belief is demonstrated in actions. So the indicator has been reworded to describe observable actions — "maintains . . ., keeps records . . ., and does not share. . . ."

The third and fifth indicators are specific, behavioral statements of outcome. They remain as originally worded. The fourth indicator again describes a *learning process,* not an outcome. Studies, investigates, researches, or other similar terms might have been used, but they would still describe learning processes. As with the first indicator, the question remains what the reason is for learning about informed consent? What should one be able to do as a result of that learning? One might be able to list the principles and processes, to conduct one's practice in ways that are consistent with those principles, or to advocate for informed consent. We chose the latter as the indicator, but you might prefer some other outcome. The essential point is that your statement describe a performance that indicates some specific outcome.

Try one final exercise to check your understanding of objectives and indicators.

2.   Improves fiscal management skills. _____

    2.1 Practices preparing program _____
       budgets. _____

    2.2 Understands the accounting _____
       processes of the agency. _____

    2.3 Is able to use monthly moni- _____
       toring reports to project ex- _____
       penditures for remainder of _____
       fiscal year. _____

    2.4 Formulates alternative fiscal _____
       plans to avoid under/over _____
       expenditures. _____

When you have finished making the corrections, compare your answers with ours on the following page.

| | |
|---|---|
| 2. Improves fiscal management skills. | Demonstrates fiscal management skills. |
| 2.1 Practices preparing program budgets. | Prepares program budgets. |
| 2.2 Understands the accounting processes of the agency. | Explains the accounting processes of the agency. |
| 2.3 Is able to use monthly monitoring reports to project expenditures for remainder of fiscal year. | Uses monthly monitoring reports to project expenditures for remainder of fiscal year |
| 2.4 Formulates alternative fiscal plans to avoid under/over expenditures. | OK |

The objective is stated as a learning process — to improve. As we observed earlier, there is no way to tell what improvement is unless there is a "base performance" level and an "ending performance" level. "Improves" is a process word, not an outcome word. So the corrected form changes "improves" to "demonstrates" or some similar term.

Similarly, in the first indicator, "practices" is a learning process and not an outcome. One practices in order to be able to do the task.

In second indicator, "understands" represents too high a level of generality. It is appropriate for an objective but not for an indicator. The specific behavioral demonstration of understanding that serves as an indicator is "explaining."

Following Gronlund's admonition to avoid unnecessary words such as "to be able to," the revision of indicator three is simply the elimination of those words. The fourth indicator is appropriately worded and needs no revision.

By now you should have a good grasp of writing objectives and indicators and should be ready to proceed to writing learning activities. Two other issues require comment before we move on.

The first issue concerns the number of indicators required to give a *representative sample* of the behaviors that are needed to fulfill each objective. Gronlund provides a helpful guideline when he says that the list of indicators is only a sample, which cannot be comprehensive, yet a careful reading of the statements should yield a fairly clear indication of what students should be like when they have achieved the objective. But some of the complex objectives we named could well have used a longer list of indicators to make the intended outcome clear. Simpler objectives may not need four indicators. The important point is that there should be a *representative sample* — "comprehensive enough to clarify the instructional intent and short enough to be manageable and useful" (Gronlund, 1970, p. 14).

The other issue is an obvious one, namely assuring that the *indicators are relevant to the objective*. Again, while this may *seem* simple, it is not uncommon to make mistakes. Gronlund gives the example of the objective of "understanding." Listing information is an indicator of a "knowledge" objective, whereas the ability to explain or use or apply is an indicator of an "understanding" objective. He urges that "knowledge" and "understanding" objectives be listed separately so that it is clear which the student is being asked to demonstrate (p. 15).

## WRITING LEARNING ACTIVITIES

Learning activities are all those experiences and tasks undertaken in order to achieve learning objectives. Learning activity statements describe what the student will do to achieve the results specified in the goal, objective, and indicator statements. We have combined the objective and indicators in one of our exercises with their implied goal to create the following example. Remember that this is only one objective among a number that would be required to achieve the goal, and only a sample of the possible indicators and learning activities associated with this objective.

*GOAL A: To be an effective social worker with families.*

OBJECTIVE A:1

Assesses family functioning using a systemic perspective.

*Indicators*

A:1.1 Specifies implicit rules of behavior in the family.

A:1.2 Identifies functional and dysfunctional communication patterns in families.

A:1.3 Describes the effect of each family member's behavior

on the family group.
The related learning activities might then include the following:
*Learning Activities*

A:1.a Read two books on family communication patterns (list the titles).

A:1.b Identify the major points in the reading material in a discussion with the field instructor.

A:1.c Observe experienced social workers in at least ten sessions and after each session describe to the social worker your perceptions of the family's functioning.

A:1.d Participate as a coworker in an average of five sessions with four different families and have debriefing sessions with the coworker following each session.

A:1.e Serve as primary or as solo social worker in an average of five sessions with two different families; audio-tape the sessions and have critique sessions with the field instructor on at least four tapes.

A:1.f Make a case presentation to an agency staff development meeting, focusing specifically on the issue of the functioning and dysfunctioning of family communication.

Writing learning activities is the easiest part of writing learning contracts. It is the part that specifies what the student is going to *do* — the actual experiences and tasks the student will have — as opposed to the goals/objectives/indicators that conceptualize the *purpose* for doing those things. However, because it is easy, there is a tendency to be less thorough than is in the best interest of the student. This section of the contract is the "job description," so to speak. The list of learning activities should be as comprehensive as possible. It should include items such as reading, researching, writing, observing, participating in meetings, making presentations, practicing specific skills, charting agency and interagency structures, recording activities, e.g., audio- or videotaping or writing verbatim transcripts, process recording, case notes, or reports.

In your statements include minimum or maximum numbers for each type of learning experience, e.g., a minimum of five marriage counseling cases or a maximum of twenty discharge planning cases. The idea is to assure enough of each kind of experience to develop a specified level of each skill while safeguarding against excessive repetition that prevents moving on to new learning.

The activities should reflect movement from the observer role to the autonomous practitioner role. In some cases it is helpful to include timetables, e.g., how long you will be observing, how long you will be a coworker, when you will start independent work, or how long you will work in each unit of the agency, such as different services of a hospital. Learning activity statements should specify what kind of recording will be done for field instruction and evaluation.

The learning activities segments of the contract should provide for time spent in study of case records and for consultation and research on problems and issues that arise during placement. For example, if students are doing marriage counseling and the couple turn out to have a sexual problem beyond their expertise, they will need time to consult experienced professionals and to read about the problem and intervention strategies.

Activities are *not* stated as behavioral outcomes, but they *are* stated in behavioral terms, e.g., "Read Minuchin's *Families and Family Therapy.*" They should be stated as specifically as possible to avoid ambiguity. For example, the above activity statement might have been written as "Read a book on family therapy." The student might responsibly carry out the activity by reading Jay Haley's *Leaving Home,* only to discover that the field instructor is not happy with the book selected. A second example of an ambiguous activity statement is "Discuss the book with the field instructor." Again, the student might be dismayed to discover that what the instructor expected was a presentation of the information acquired from the book as well as an assessment of the implications for the student's social work practice.

The student and field instructor use the preparation of the contract to clarify expectations and to learn. If the point of a given activity is that the student understand basic principles of structural family therapy and consider consequent practice implications, then the statement should so specify. The activity statements might then read:

1. Read Salvador Minuchin's *Families and Family Therapy.*
2. Present to the field instructor the major points of the book, questions resulting from reading the book, ideas stimulated

by the reading, and ideas about how the concepts and ideas in the book are likely to affect practice.

The point is simply this: the activities need to be stated in as un-ambiguous terms as possible. The expected behaviors should be-clearly specified in the learning activity statements. It is more likely that the objective will be reached if the activities are carefully de-signed and clearly specified. Moreover, lack of clarity may lead to frustrations and hard feelings between student and instructor.

Check your understanding of the appropriate content for learn-ing activity statements. Circle the statement(s) below that is(are) correctly worded:

1. Receive feedback from parent about results.
2. Write a brochure describing an agency program.
3. Learn the NASW Code of Ethics.

If you are clear on the way to state a learning activity, you identified the second statement as correctly worded and both the first and third as too ambiguous. In the first statement it is not clear what kind of "feedback" is requested. Is it information or evaluation? The activity might be stated as "Obtain information from the parents of the changes that followed intervention" or "Obtain parent's evaluation of the effectiveness of the intervention." Similarly, in the third statement, the verb "learn" could refer to a variety of specific behaviors. It might mean "read" or "memorize" or "apply to specific cases." Again, an activity should refer to a particular behavior.

The following is a list of learning activity statements. As in previous exercises, if the statement is correct as written, write "OK" in the space to the right of the statement. If the statement is not correct as written, use the space to the right to revise the statement. (In some cases a statement that is too general will need to be broken into two or more activities in order to achieve useful behavioral specificity.)

1.  Help citizens change an agency policy.

2.  Conduct ten intake interviews.

3.  Gain knowledge of interorganizational linkages among mental health agencies.

4.  Improve case-recording skills.

_____
_____
_____
_____
5.  Teach parenting skills      _____
    as a ten session            _____
    seminar to a group of       _____
    ten to fifteen single       _____
    parents.                    _____
                                _____
                                _____

Once you have made your judgments and revised those statements that you believe are incorrect, please proceed to our suggestions and comments on the following page.

| | | |
|---|---|---|
| 1. | Help citizens change an agency policy. | Assist citizens in calling a meeting to discuss common problems. Encourage meeting participants to clarify the source of the problem(s) and to identify specific policies that underlie it (them). |
| 2. | Conduct ten intake interviews. | OK |
| 3. | Gain knowledge of inter-organizational linkages among mental health agencies. | Interview key persons in MH agencies re: their understandings and percep-tions of interorganizational linkages. Summarize findings to field instructor who will clarify any confusions and state any differences in understand-ing or perception. |
| 4. | Improve case-recording skills. | Write case notes in all case records. Meet with field instructor to assess recording skills. |
| 5. | Teach parenting skills as a ten session seminar to a group of ten to fifteen single parents. | OK |

The first activity statement is incorrect because it specifies an outcome (objective), not a learning process. The desired outcome is that citizens learn to make changes in agency policies. There are many activities that would be necessary to the achievement of such an objective, and our revisions represent only a sample of the possible activities. Note the limited scope and the specificity of each of the suggested activities.

The second activity is OK as written. It describes a specific action and even includes the number of times it will occur.

The third activity statement is vague. It does not explain what activities are necessary. We have suggested two possible activities that might accomplish the desired end. You may have written others, which is fine, as long as they describe specific behaviors.

The fourth statement does not describe an activity, though there is an implied intent. The activities are "writing" and having the writing assessed. Note in both this and the previous list that an *activity of the field instructor* is included. These are usually activities related to assessing the student's performance; it is important that they be included so that the expectations for the field instructor's performance are clear as well.

The last activity is OK as written. It tells what the student is supposed to do (teach a seminar) and even specifies the number of sessions, the number of persons in the group, and the characteristics of the group members.

A number of verbs are commonly used in writing activity statements: prepare, write, present, interview, observe, review, study, simulate, work as, counsel, participate in, accompany, make, contact, listen to, tape, formulate, teach, attend, research, assist, train, and summarize. This is, of course, simply a sample. Many others verbs are equally appropriate.

Before we proceed, a word of caution. Though the distinctions between the elements of the learning contract may seem clear and simple in a prepared text such as this, the boundaries between indicators and activities are not always evident. There are some activities that, when written in a different form, are also indicators. For example, an objective might be "Demonstrates grant development skills" and the indicators might include "Writes program description" and "Drafts budget." The activities related to this objective might include items such as the following:

1. Read the RFP (request for proposal) received from the agency director.
2. Telephone official at funding agency for detailed information.
3. Research the literature on the topic.
4. Interview appropriate agency program personnel to learn their interests and ideas for a grant proposal.
5. Consult with the finance director about agency require-

ments for grant budgets.

6. Draft and distribute outline of narrative and skeleton budget.
7. Lead discussion about proposal with agency personnel.
8. Write grant proposal narrative.
9. Prepare budget.
10. Submit budget to fiscal director for review/approval/revision.
11. Submit narrative to director and to all involved program personnel for review/approval/revision.
12. Make revisions as recommended.
13. Mail grant to funding agency.

Note that writing the narrative (#8 above) and drafting the budget (#9 above) are two of the *activities* involved in the achievement of the objective. Writing the narrative and drafting the budget are *indicators* also. Such overlap is inevitable because some activities describe the preparation of products. However, most of the activities are steps that must precede the actual preparation of those products.

### WRITING EVALUATION PLANS

The final step in writing a learning contract is to describe the evaluation plans, i.e., the procedure and criteria for assessment. This requires answering four questions:

*Who* will make the assessment?

*What data* will be used?

*What criteria* (quantitative and qualitative) will be applied?

*When* will it occur?

WHO? Primary responsibility for assessment usually rests with the field instructor. However, achievement of certain objectives will be best assessed by other professional staff in the field setting, by classmates or faculty (for example, when one of the products related to an objective is presented in a field seminar), by clients, or by some combination of persons.

WHAT DATA? The question is what sources of information will be used to evaluate progress. There are at least five types of data that may be used:

*Direct observation of interactional processes* (live, audio-tape, or videotape), e.g.,

> in-office sessions or visits to homes for either clinical or organizational functions;
>
> meetings — staff, interagency, neighborhood committees, task forces;
>
> interactions with professional colleagues and agency support staff.

*Observation of the form and content of documents,* e.g.,

| | |
|---|---|
| case histories, | budgets, |
| case records, | organizational charts, |
| home studies, | program evaluation reports, |
| court reports | funding proposals, |
| referral summaries, | fact-finding reports, |
| verbatims, | policy proposals, |
| process recordings, | activity reports, |

> investigative reports on a community issue,
>
> analysis of an agency problem.

*Students' subjective reports,* e.g.,

> self-awareness and perceptions about interactions conveyed through a process recording, a case record, or an activity report;
>
> understanding of the politics and processes of an organization represented in an organizational chart.

*Reports of the perceptions of others,* e.g.,

> colleagues,
>
> clients,
>
> community citizens.

*Agency information system statistics,* e.g.,

> number of cases opened and closed,
>
> number of contacts,
>
> length of treatment,
>
> number of neighborhood meetings held,
>
> number of people attending meetings.

Clarity about what data will be used is essential. A variety of types of data contributes to a comprehensive assessment of student performance.

WHAT CRITERIA? As noted earlier, indicators are "performances that give evidence of capacities." Thus indicators provide the gross criteria for judging whether each objective has been accomplished. Finer discriminations abut how well the objective has been accomplished require judgments about both the quantity and quality of the evidence. The minimum quantities acceptable as evidence of accomplishment are spelled out in the learning activity statements. Judging the quality of performance remains the major difficulty in assessing complex learning objectives. Judgments of quality are inescapably subjective and virtually impossible to define in a written contract.

While the learning contract makes evaluation a less arbitrary process, it does not eliminate altogether the subjective element of evaluation. The objectives clarify *what outcomes* will be evaluated; the indicators clarify *what performances* will provide evidence of the extent to which the objectives have been achieved; and the activities delineate the *tasks that will be accomplished* in moving toward the objective. But the fact that the student has done all the tasks does not necessarily mean that the student has *achieved* the competency specified in the objective. A judgment is still required to determine whether the quality of the performance on the specific activities indicates the achievement of — or a reasonable degree of progress toward — the objective.

One of the potential problems with learning contracts is that students — and sometimes field instructors and faculty members as well — may assume that an objective has been achieved when all of the activities have been completed, and that qualitative judgments have been eliminated by the learning contract. Consequently, students may express frustration and anger when they believe they have successfully achieved an objective and the field instructor or faculty coordinator does not agree.

This problem can be illustrated by the following everyday example. If a father assigns his son the dish washing and kitchen cleanup, he could use various criteria to assess his son's performance. The father may judge that some dishes are not as clean as he thinks they should be, or that soap has not been rinsed off thoroughly, or that stove and countertops have not been wiped sparkling clean. As a result, he might insist that the job be done again. When confronted by the father, the son may protest that all the dishes were scrubbed in the dish water and sprayed with rinse water, and that the stove and countertops were wiped off. The disagreement is only apparently about whether the son performed all assigned tasks and thus reached the objective. The real issue is that there was an unspecified criterion, that is, a given quality of performance, that was applied by the father.

It would be possible, at least theoretically, for the father to specify all the criteria he planned to use to evalute his son's performance. They might include, for example, that the dishes be free of food particles and soap film. On different days the father might vary regarding the rigor with which he judged the performance, but a least the criteria would be clear — until the son broke six dishes and the father realized the need to add another criterion.

While this problem cannot be entirely resolved, it can be alleviated. We have said earlier that it is impossible to list all the indicators or criteria for any objective, especially if the objective describes a complex competency. There are even problems in clearly stating all the criteria for an objective such as washing dishes. When the objective has to do with clinical skills or supevisory skills or other complex behavior, it is much more difficult to specify evaluation criteria. However, explicitness, a characteristic of a valid contract, requires that all expectations be made clear. Since subjective criteria cannot be definitively written, we urge two procedures: (1) the inclusion of a general statement indicating that part of the evaluation will be subjective judgments of the quality of performance, and (2) frequent evaluation conferences between student and field instructor to insure that subjective expectations become clear.

Our experience is that, in addition to weekly meetings of the student and field instructor, formal periodic evaluation sessions with the faculty coordinator are essential to the specification of subjective criteria and to qualitative evaluation. Prior to these sessions both field instructor and student prepare written narrative evaluations. This evaluation process identifies those objectives where good progress is being made and those where progress is insufficient. It allows for an analysis of what needs to be done to improve performance. This may lead to increased focus on an objective, changes in the instructional process, increased or altered learning activities, improved evaluation techniques, or modifications in the objectives themselves. Whatever the corrective action taken to facilitate progress, the subjective criteria should become clearer and the student should have a better understanding of what is needed and expected in order to achieve the objectives.

Arthur Chickering (1977) suggests that, when an instructor is writing a narrative evaluation of a student, the evaluation should have two components.

> The most effective evaluation gives a judgment and then describes the behavior, products, evidences on which the judgment rests. This combination is powerful because it combines telling with showing. The reader, whether student, faculty, or outside agency, not only is told the opinion of the judge but also gets information which shows what actually was done.
>
> When this approach is used . . . the evaluation of the contract can be seen as a balance among the various strengths and weaknesses, and as a junction of the judgments about the elements. The key thing is to be clear when we are simply describing what happened and presenting evidence, and when we are rendering a judgment. (p. 99)

Malcolm Knowles emphasizes the qualitative nature of evaluation and cautions against movements toward quantifiable evaluation in professional education. He encourages thinking less in terms of evaluation and more in terms of "rediagnosis."

> At the end of a learning experience I engage my students in reexamining their models of required competencies and reassessing their levels of development. Two things happen: they discover that they have raised their levels of aspiration regarding the required competencies and that new gaps have appeared between where they are now and where they want to be in their development. Rediagnosis thus builds in the notion of continuing learning, which I think the static concept of evaluation largely destroys. (p. 39)

WHEN? As suggested above, evaluation is an ongoing activity. Field education, as preparation for practice, is an intensive time of learning. Frequent assessment is critical to the student's learning and personal growth. The learning contract is an aid for guiding education. It is not simply a document for making a final judgment of the student's competence for entry into the profession. Thus the evaluation plan should specify both the frequency of student-instructor conferences and the timetable for written assessments and formal evaluation sessions with both instructor and faculty coordinator. (If the frequency of written assessments and formal evaluation sessions that include the faculty coordinator is established policy and is stated elsewhere, such as in a field education handbook distributed to students and field instructors, then it does not need to be specified in the learning contract.)

The following are examples of evaluation process statements that answer the four questions we have just discussed. The first is an evaluation statement that might follow the objective "Assesses family functioning using a systemic perspective" and the related indicators and learning activities in the example on pages 109-110.

> EVALUATION: Assessment will be done by the field instructor in weekly conferences with the student based on live observation of cowork; audiotapes, process recordings, and the case presentation of solo work; and discussion of readings. Qualitative judgments will be central elements of assessment in the weekly conferences and in written narratives submitted to an discussed with the faculty coordinator twice each semester.

The second example is an evaluation statement that might follow the objective "Improves fiscal management skills" (see page 108).

> EVALUATION: Field instructor and agency fiscal manager will assess progress in periodic conference with the student based on written documents such as budgets and fiscal reports prepared by student, and presentations and discussions in conferences. Evaluation will include qualitative judgments. Written narrative assessments will be prepared and submitted to the faculty coordinator prior to the visits as scheduled in the *Field Education Handbook*.

The third example is an evaluation statement that might follow the objective "Organizes neighborhood residents to solve a problem that negatively affects their community" (see pages 99-101).

> EVALUATION: Field instructor will evaluate progress in weekly sessions with student based on student activ-

ity reports; live observation of telephone communi-
cations, conversations with public officials, visits in
homes, planning meetings, and neighborhood meetings; information and analysis in issue investigation
report; reports from community leadership; and discussions of strategies and implementation plans.
Qualitative considerations will be part of the assessment in weekly sessions and in narratives written in
preparation for once-per-semester evaluation sessions with the faculty coordinator.

Note that all three examples answer the four questions:

*Who?* — field instructor, except in the second example, where the fiscal manager is included:

*What data?* — selected on the basis of relevance to the particular objective, indicators, and activities;

*What criteria?* — indicators and activities are already specified, so
statements are included about the qualitative dimension;

*When?* — weekly or periodic conferences depending on appropriateness to the objective, plus meetings with the faculty coordinator at
specified intervals.

## CONCLUSION

You are ready to write your own learning contract. However,
writing the contract is not just a mechanical process. Learning contracts are tools that can facilitate communication about the field education experience. The process of developing the contract
encourages a quantity and quality of exchange that is important to
the attainment of educational goals. The contract serves to clarify
long-term and short-term expectations and to specify in some detail
the commitments of various parties. However, contracts are not
ends in themselves. Flexibility is a crucial element in their creation
and use. The purpose of learning contracts within the context of humanist education is defeated if they inhibit rather than enable.

# REFERENCES

Chickering, A.W. Evaluation in the context of contract learning. *Journal of Personalized Instruction*, 1977, *2*, 96-100.

Finestone, S. Selected features of professional field instruction. In B.L. Jones (Ed.), *Current patterns in field instruction in graduate social work education.* New York: Council on Social Work Education, 1969.

Gronlund, N.E. *Stating behavioral objectives for classroom instruction.* New York: Macmillan, 1970.

Knowles, M.S. Innovations in teaching styles and approaches based upon adult learning. *Journal of Education for Social Work*, 1972, *8*(2), 32-39.

Popham, W.J. Instructional objectives 1960-1970. *Improving Human Performance: A Research Quarterly*, 1973, *3*, 191-198.

Pratt, D. Humanistic goals and behavior objectives: Toward a synthesis. *Journal of Curriculum Studies*, 1976, *8*, 15-25.

# NAME INDEX

## A

Adelman, H., 56, 57, 74, 77
Armitage, A., 67, 71, 77
Atkin, J.M., 70-71

## B

Baer, B., 36-37, 51
Barlow, R., 71-72, 77
Becker, L., 72, 73, 77
Bernstein, B., 71, 77
Berte, R., 54, 59, 78
Bigge, M., 60, 78
Blackey, E., 14, 46, 51
Bloom, B., 20, 51, 61, 78, 79
Boland, M., 24-25, 51-52
Bower, G., 60, 78
Briar, S., 46-47, 52
Brigham, T., 56, 78
Brownstein, C., 47, 52
Bruner, J., 60, 78
Bryan, J., 60, 72, 73, 79
Burns, R., 61, 78

## C

Chickering, A., 71-72, 78, 122, 125
Clark, F., 67, 71, 77
Cleghorn, J., 59, 78
Colby, I., 57, 71, 78
Coles, R., 55, 78
Council on Social Work Education, 19-20, 21, 29, 52

## D

Dana, B., 12, 46-47, 52
Dewey, J., 54, 60, 63, 78

DeYoung, A., 20-21, 22, 41, 53
Diamonti, M., 65, 66-67, 68, 70, 78
Dinerman, M., 10, 29, 52
Dossett, D., 72, 73, 79
Duchastel, P., 72, 78

## E

Englehart, M., 20, 51, 61, 78
Ezell, B., 67, 80

## F

Federico, R., 36-37, 51
Finestone, S., 82, 125
Flanigan, B., 57, 78
Fortune, A., 48, 52
Freire, P., 54, 56, 58, 60, 78
Furst, E., 20, 51, 61, 78

## G

Gaa, J., 72, 73, 78
Garrard, V., 3, 9
Germain, C., 36-37, 52
Gilbert, J., 57, 58, 78
Goldman, G., 71, 78
Gronlund, N., 65-66, 74-75, 78, 91-95, 108, 125
Grossman, C., 21, 52

## H

Hale, M., 12, 52
Hamilton, M., 3, 9, 46-47, 52
Hartwig, J., 57-58, 78
Hilgard, E., 60, 78
Hill, W., 20, 51, 61, 78
Hockenstad, M., 56-57, 58, 78

Holt, J., 55, 78, 79
Houpt, J., 59, 79

**I**
Illich, I., 55, 79
Ivancevich, J., 67-68, 72, 79

**J**
Johnson, H., 24-25, 51-52
Jones, B., 32, 52
Jones, W., 10, 53

**K**
Kindelsperger, W., 14, 52
Knowles, M., 54, 55-56, 58, 60, 79, 122, 125
Koegler, R., 21-22, 52
Kozol, J., 55, 79
Krathwohl, D., 20, 51, 61, 78, 79

**L**
LaComte, C., 71, 77
Latham, G., 72, 73, 79
Lehmann, T., 71-72, 79
Leight, R., 63, 79
Levin, S., 59, 78
Locke, E., 72-73, 79

**M**
McAshan, H., 61, 80
MacDonald-Ross, M., 61, 79
McMahon, J., 67-68, 72, 79
McNew, E., 20-21, 22, 41, 53
Mager, R., 61, 66, 79
Maier, H., 11, 52
Maluccio, A., 74, 79-80
Marlow, W., 74, 79-80
Masia, B., 61, 79
Matson, M., 12-13, 18, 19-20, 23, 52
Melton, R., 72, 74, 80
Merrill, P., 72, 78
Meyer, C., 36-37, 53
Minahan, A., 36-37, 53

Mitchell, T., 72, 73, 79
Murphy, S., 65, 66-67, 68, 70, 78

**N**
Nelson, J., 63, 66, 68, 70, 80

**P**
Pincus, A., 36-37, 53
Popham, W., 61, 65-66, 74, 80, 91, 125
Pratt, D., 61-62, 64, 65, 67, 75, 80, 91, 125
Press, A., 20-21, 53

**R**
Regensberg, J., 12, 15, 53
Rigby, B., 56-57, 58, 78
Rothman, J., 10, 53
Russell, M., 59, 79

**S**
Schubert, M., 13-14, 18-20, 41, 53
Seabury, B., 71, 74, 77, 80
Shenkman, H., 69, 71, 74, 80
Shumate, N., 63, 70, 80
Sikemma, M., 12-13, 16, 18-19, 20, 22, 53
Somers, M., 60, 80
Streidl, J., 67-68, 79
Szilagyi, A., 67-68, 79

**T**
Taylor, L., 56, 57, 74, 77
Thomas, G., 67, 80
Towle, C., 20, 53
Tyler, R., 14, 53, 60, 61, 80

**W**
Wedel, K., 20-21, 53
Weinstein, H., 59, 79
Westbury I., 59, 64-65, 80
Williamson, E., 21, 52

**Y**
Yuhl, G., 72, 73, 79

# SUBJECT INDEX

**A**

Accountability, 7, 68, 70
Accreditation, 29
Activities (*see* Learning activities)
Agency, 5-9, 12, 16, 32-33, 35, 45, 46-47, 49-50
Alinsky, S., 44
Andragogy, 55
Apprenticeship, 12-13
Aristotle, 55
Assessment (*see* Criteria)
Attitudes (*see* Values)
Autonomous practice, 11, 15, 22
Autonomy, 16-17

**B**

Behaviorist perspective
    humanist education, incongruence
        with, 61-71

**C**

Casework (*see* Methods of practice)
Change, 57, 58, 62, 99
    personal, 62
    social, 14-15
Cicero, 55
Commitment, 6-7, 76
Community organization (*see* Methods of practice)
Component, 3-5, 10, 15, 83
Conformity, 70-71
Confucius, 55
Content, 11, 15, 21, 82-84 (*see also* Indicators; Learning Contracts; learning objectives)

Content generality, 66, 75, 91
Continuity, 14-15
Contract (*see* Learning contract)
Contracting, 57-59
Creativity, 21-22, 57, 70-71, 75
Credit, 10
Criteria, 7
    assessment, 50, 67, 71, 82, 118 (*see also* Evaluation, plans)
Critical inquiry, 63, 66
Curriculum, 10-11, 13-17, 51, 82
    design, 23, 24, 86
    field education, 8, 17, 46
    organization, 88, 90
    social work, 3, 11, 14, 60, 82, 86-87, 88

**D**

Data, 118-120
Direct instruction, 17, 42-43
Direct observation, 17, 42, 119
Diversity, 75, 83
    classroom, field education relationship, 20-21
    field instruction, 31
    of discipline, 37
    of experience, 30
    of population served, 33, 37-38
Dynamic, 74
Dynamism, 76-77, 82

**E**

Education
    nature of, 62-65
    social work, 13-14, 58-59

Educational process, 12
Empowerment viii, 5, 56-58
Equity, 16
Euclid, 55
Evaluation, 6-7, 74, 75-76, 81
    plans, 82, 118-124
Explicit, 74
Explicitness, 75-76, 82

**F**
Faculty involvement, 6-8, 16, 40-41, 50-51
Feedback, 59, 72
Field education, 3-5, 10-51, 60
    ambivalence toward,
        by field instructors, 4
        by social work educators, 3-4
        by students, 4
    contributions of, 17
    credit hours, 10
    definition, 11-13
    educational focus, 12, 13, 15-16
    educational responsibility, 8, 46, 47
    goals, 14, 17-20
    lack of consensus concerning, 4-5
    objectives of, 17-20
    preparation, 3
    principles of, 13-17
    structure of, 23-32
    uniqueness of, 15-16
    view of, 3-4
Field experience (*see* Field education)
Field instruction, 16-17, 35
    number of students jointly, 34, 41
    source, 34, 39-41
    teaching format, 34, 41-42
    teaching methods, 34, 43-44
Field instructor, 4, 6, 8-9, 34-35, 39-40, 43-45, 49
Field learning (*see* Field education)
Fields of practice, 37-38, 86-87, 90 (*see also* Social problems)
Field teaching (*see* Field education)
Field work, 3-4 (*see also* Field education)
Flexibility, 22
Formality, 74-75, 82
Format, 24-28, 58-59, 74-75, 91
    teaching, 34, 41-42 (*see aslo* Learning contract)

**G**
Generalization, 16-17
Goals, 71-73
    definition, 75, 81, 84, 87
    educational, 59
    examples of, 84-85, 86, 109-110
    goal phasing, 89
    self-testing opportunities, 87, 89, 90
    writing, 84-91 (*see also* Field Education; Learning; Learning contract)

**H**
Haley, J., 105
Hierarchy, 85-86, 88-90
    design, 86
Human behavior, 14-15
Human behavior in the social environment, 82
Humanist perspective, vii, 5, 74
    education, 54-59

**I**
Indicators, 66, 67, 75, 81-82, 91-109
    behavioral verbs, 91
    definition, 91
    examples, 86, 95, 97, 109-110
    self-testing opportunities, 92, 93, 96, 98-99, 107
Individualization, viii, 5, 30, 60, 71, 76, 82, 84
Innovation, 33, 39, 63
Integration, 15, 18-22, 25
Interdisciplinary, 33, 37
Internship (*see* Field education)
Intervention, 86
Interview, 6

**J**
Jesus, 55
Johnson, H. Wayne, vii

**K**
Knowledge, 15, 17-22, 56
Kruse, Katherine, vii

**L**
Lao Tse, 55
Learning
    cognitive, 21

conceptual, 12, 17, 27, 28
continuous, 19
deductive, 12, 27-28
experiences, 15
experiential, 27
goal, 6
inductive, 12, 27
modes of, 14
modules, 40
needs, 6
opportunities, 6-7, 11, 16, 32-33, 35-39
styles, 6
theory, 59-60
Learning activities, 6-7, 74-75, 76, 82, 109-118
active verbs, 117
definition, 109
examples, 110, 111-113, 117-118
expected behaviors, 113
self-testing opportunities, 113-116
Learning contracts, 5-8, 54-77, 81-125
benefits of, 9, 59-61
characteristics, 82
content of, 82-84
definitions, 54, 81-82
educational focus, 5-6, 54-55
educational intents, diagram, 86
elements of, 81-82
field education, 60-61
format of, 58-59, 75, 81-82
functions of, 5-8
goals, 6, 81, 85-86
misconceptions, 60
research findings, 71-74
tools, 8
valid, 74-77
Learning objectives, 81, 84, 87, 91-105
active verbs, 91
content of, 93
definition, 87, 91
examples, 86, 101, 109
self-testing opportunities, 87, 93, 95, 99, 103, 104, 107

**M**
Methods of practice, 33, 36-37
Minuchin, S., 111
Mutual, 60, 74

Mutuality, 60, 76, 82

**N**
Negotiation, 57-59, 70-71, 82
Nonsexist, viii

**O**
Objectives, 6, 72, 74-75, 76
behavioral, 61-62, 64-67, 68, 69, 73-74
educational, 63, 67
experiential, 64
instructional, 61, 62, 65-66
knowledge, 20-22
learning (*see* Learning objectives)
skill, 18-19, 22-23
value, 19, 23, 85-86 (*see also* Field education; learning contracts)
Outcomes
self-testing opportunities, 110

**P**
Pedagogy, 55-56
Performance criteria, 65, 75, 91
Placement, 5-6, 13, 23-32, 35-36
block, 24-28
concurrent, 24-28
processes, 47-50
typologies, 32
Plato, 55
Policy, 15 (*see also* Social policy)
Postservice review, 17, 42-43
Practice, 11, 15, 17, 82
generic, 83
macro, viii, 86
method, 83, 86, 88, 90
micro, viii, 86
professional, 22
skills, 7, 18
social work, 22
strategies, 23
techniques, 23
Practicum (*see* Field education)
Praxis, 58
Problem solving, 14-15, 22, 63
Process, 97-99, 104-105, 108, 123-124
self-testing opportunities, 97
Professionalism, 13, 18-20, 70
professional education, 13-14, 82
professional identity, 20, 64, 88

professional practice, 13, 15, 22, 64-65, 66-67
professional relationships, 22-23
Progression, 15

**Q**
Quantification, 67-69
Quintilian, 55

**R**
Realism, 77, 82
Realistic, 74
Reciprocal, 74
Reciprocity, 76, 82
Reductionism, 67-68
Representative sample, 75, 91, 108
Research, 13-15, 82
Rigidity, 70-71, 74
Roles, 18, 19-20, 58, 69, 83

**S**
Self-awareness, 14-15, 18-19, 23
Sequences, 15, 82-84
Service area, 33, 37
Skills, 7, 12, 15, 17, 19, 56
Social policy, 11, 82
Social problems, 18, 33, 36, 83, 87-88

Social work programs
    expectations, 5-6
    goals, 6, 85
    graduate, 10, 20, 24-32
    rational, 6
    undergraduate, 10, 20, 24-32
Socrates, 55
Specialization, 83-84
Structure (*see* Field education)
System levels, 86 (*see also* Agency)
Systems perspective, 14-15

**T**
Teaching centers, 32-33, 35
Teaching methods, 34, 42-43
Teaching unit, 41
Theoretical orientation
    of agency, 33, 36
    of field instructor, 34, 43
Training, 62
Transferability, 16-17

**V**
Values
    objectives, 23
    social work, 5, 15, 19, 54, 59-60
Volunteerism, 28-29